Keep Me Travelling

Henry Ormerod

© Henry Ormerod 2006
KEEP ME TRAVELLING
ISBN 0-9552253-0-2

Published by:
Ridercross Publications
5 Waterloo Drive
Banbury
Oxon
OX16 3QN

The right of Henry Ormerod to be identified as the author of this work has been asserted by him in accordance with the Copyright, Design and Patent Act 1988.

All rights reserved. No part of this publication may be produced in any form or by any means – graphic, electronic or mechanical including photocopying, taping or information storage and retrieval systems – without the prior permission, in writing, of the publisher.

Cover design by Priscilla Ormerod

Design and production co-ordinated by:
The ***Better Book*** Company Ltd
Forum House
Stirling Road
Chichester
PO19 7DN

Contents

Acknowledgements v
Introduction vii

1. Prams and Trams 1

2. Buses, Cars, Steam Trains and My Own Two Feet 4

3. Bicycles, the Latest Modern Post-War Buses, the Old
   Steam Trains again, and more Daimlers 15

4. Troop Carriers, My Own Two Feet in Boots, more Steam
   Trains, "Express" 30 mph Coaches, and a Sea Voyage ... 24

5. London Transport Buses and Tubes, Electric and Diesel
   BR Trains, Two-Wheels Leg-Powered and Petrol-Powered ... 51

6. Wedding Car, Aircraft, Priscilla's Simca 65

7. Austins, Hondas, InterCity 125s, the "National
   Bus Company" 78

8. Motorways, Several Aircraft, Cross Channel Ferries 107

9. Horses; Troublesome drives via Syresham; Introduction
   to the Stagecoach Empire; "Super-Sprinters" 129

10. Park-and-Ride; Virgin, Chiltern and Thames Trains;
    Foreign Underground Systems; "Once a Week"
    Bus Services 153

11. "Keep me Travelling ..." 168

12. "... Along With You." 183

Acknowledgements

"Keep Me Travelling"

"It's from the old I travel to the new;
Keep me travelling along with you."
SYDNEY CARTER.

For

Claire and Kevin

With every good wish

Henry Ormerod

Introduction

When anyone writes a book, he or she presumably has some idea of the intended readership. I had better come clean straight away, and say that I hope this volume will appeal to people who come into at least one of the following categories:

(a) Those interested in the religious aspects of social history since the 1930s.
(b) Those interested in the transport aspects of social history since the 1930s.
(c) Those whose paths have crossed my own since the days of the Second World War.

I can think of some people who belong to all three categories. I can think of many in categories (a) or (b) and also in (c). I believe that there are quite a number of people who belong to both categories (a) and (b), as I do. I hope that any picking up this book who belong to only one of the three categories will find sufficient in it to regard it as a worthwhile read.

The book is in the nature of an autobiography. However, the main focus is not meant to be on myself, but on what I have observed as I have travelled through life from as far back as I can remember. The chapter titles all have transport references.

CHAPTER 1

Prams and Trams

I was born in Bristol on 8 February 1935. My father was a doctor, a general practitioner, with a widespread practice around north-west Bristol, which he had inherited from his father. Some of his patients were in quite rural areas. Our home was at the northern extremity of Durdham Downs, about three miles from the city centre. My father, Dr George Lawrence Ormerod, always known as Lawrence, had a surgery in what I remember from boyhood days as being referred to as the "village" of Westbury-on-Trym, as well as a surgery in his own house. During the Second World War he was doing the work of three doctors; and at night he was often firewatching with the ARP, and on duty at Avonmouth Docks. My mother, Violet Reid Ormerod (née Paterson) came from Edinburgh, where her father, The Very Revd William Paterson (of the Church of Scotland) had been Professor of Divinity at the University.

Some of my earliest memories are of the Bristol trams, which passed our house frequently. They were very antiquated even by then, and all had open seating upstairs. Many of them, I later learned, had originally been horse trams, dating from the later years of the nineteenth century. The city tramways had been electrified in 1900. Tram rides are much more vivid in my memory than pram rides. In May, 1938, when I was aged three, the trams on our route were replaced by buses; and still I have vague memories of how different from the trams the buses seemed. The tram to bus changeover arose from the involvement of Bristol Corporation in the provision of transport in the city. For decades the Corporation could not reach agreement over purchasing from the Bristol Tramways and Carriage Company the tram system that had been inaugurated in the 1870s.

By the mid-1930s the trams had come to the end of their useful life; and the company had introduced a good many bus services on roads not served by trams. In 1936 an agreement was reached giving the Corporation a half-share in the city transport system, which continued to be managed and operated by "Bristol Tramways", a name which survived until 1957. A major scheme to rid Bristol of its old trams, and put diesel double-decker buses in their place, changed the face of Bristol over the immediate pre-war period; in fact the last trams survived into wartime, and ended their career as a result of enemy action, which destroyed a great deal of their infrastructure.

Fortunately, there were new buses waiting in the wings to enter service (tram drivers having already been trained to drive them). All the "tramway replacement" buses were built in Bristol by the Tramways Company (the plant later becoming a separate entity as "Bristol Commercial Vehicles"). They were rugged vehicles, with few refinements, but had an enviable reputation for reliability and economy. Five-cylinder Gardner engines were fitted, not ideal, one might think, for such a hilly city; but nobody seemed to mind their slow uphill progress, or their noise and vibration, and they served the city extremely well until they were replaced by new buses in the 1950s. Some pre-war buses had their lives extended by re-bodying. Incidentally, the Bristol Tramways and Carriage Company, part of the Tilling Group, which was nationalised after the war, operated a very extensive system of bus routes over much of Gloucestershire, North Somerset, and North and West Wiltshire – now shared mainly by the First and Stagecoach groups.

CHAPTER 2

Buses, Cars, Steam Trains and my own two feet.

I have clear memories of the air-raid sirens. Every house in Bristol was supposed to be within hearing range of one of them. To warn of coming raids they sounded intermittently; and the "all clear" message was an unbroken sound. We used to go into the cellar of our home for shelter; and if things seemed very bad, we took refuge in the coal hole, which my parents thought was the safest place. On quite a number of occasions we spent a large part of the night sheltering. During the mornings I attended a kindergarten school nearby, where excellent foundations of the three Rs were laid. My brother William, two years younger than myself, joined me there for the last part of my time.

However, the seriousness of the continuing blitz on Bristol led our parents to arrange for us to be evacuated, under the charge of a most delightful governess, who had earlier been employed in our family as a nanny. We both had complete confidence in her, and strong affection for her. First we went to lodge in a farmhouse at Claverham, between Bristol and Weston-super-Mare. That turned out to be too near the bombing for comfort, and the farmhouse was damaged. My chief memory of Claverham is the railway bridge, over the main Bristol to West Country line. We loved to stand on the bridge, not just to observe the frequent trains, but even more enthusiastically to study the railway signals going up and down. We named each signal after a family member or friend! I can remember the signal lay-out very clearly indeed.

Our parents transferred us to what they hoped would be a safer place, namely the delightful village of Dunster, near Minehead, on the edge of Exmoor. Our grandmother was living there at the time; and we lived, with "Nanny", the governess, in rooms nearby, for about six months in 1941. I got to know "Granny" much better during that time. She gave me an atlas, with which I was thrilled; and I learned a good deal of geography from her. I also attended the morning service at Dunster parish church with her on Sundays; and she taught me a number of hymns, and I loved it when hymns that I had learned from her came up at church – including "Onward, Christian soldiers", "Who would true valour see", and perhaps surprisingly, "All hail the power of Jesus' Name", with its "Crown Him" chorus; and that was my favourite hymn for a time. I also learned "All things bright and beautiful", which is reputed to have been inspired by a visit to Dunster paid by its author from her home in Ireland.

Dunster had a railway station on the branch line from Taunton (now the West Somerset preserved railway). The station was some way out of the village, on the way to Dunster beach; and "Nanny" arranged it that we should walk to the beach, passing the station at a time when one of the not very frequent trains was due. Occasionally we caught the train to Minehead, and once in the other direction to Watchet – short journeys, but great fun for a six-year-old. There was also the hourly Western National green single-deck bus that linked Dunster village with Minehead. For me previously buses had always been double-deckers, and it seemed funny to go on one with no upstairs!

Perhaps my most abiding memory of Dunster is the glorious countryside in walking distance from the village. "Nanny" took us on lots of walks, some quite long; and I learned from her, with the help also of books, a great deal about wild flowers, and about birds, and wild life generally. The effort of climbing the nearby hill of Grabbist was well worth it for the glorious views – and of course it was necessary for William and me to use up our plentiful energy.

I had heard the words "boarding school" used a number of times, but didn't really understand what they meant – until on Sunday, 21 September 1941 our father came along unexpectedly in the morning, whisked William and me, and presumably "Nanny" into his 1936 Daimler saloon car, and drove us back to our home at Bristol for lunch. I remember that in itself being quite a disconcerting experience; it was nine months since I had been there, a long time for a young child. However, it was a very brief visit, for after lunch we were back in the car again, not knowing where we were going. Actually, it was to "boarding school"! I was six; William was aged only four.

The school was called Rose Hill, and was situated in the small village of Alderley, close to Wotton-under-

Edge, in the Gloucestershire Cotswold country. Rose Hill had been evacuated from Banstead, Surrey, to occupy the "large house" in the village, recently vacated by the squire. William was in the infants' department, where delightful and capable Miss Clay and "Nanny Shaw" took charge of the youngest boys. As a six-year-old I was in the main school, where it was necessary to be able to tie your tie and polish your shoes and wear your uniform smartly – and wash yourself and clean your teeth and brush your hair. "Nanny" had given me a good deal of practice at Dunster.

Actually, at Rose Hill the matrons were extremely good and caring. The head matron evidently looked at the Times and Telegraph notices of births, marriages and deaths every day for years afterwards, judging from the very kind letters I received from her when I was in my thirties and forties, on the occasions of the deaths of my parents, my marriage to Priscilla (of which much more anon), and the births of our children.

The headmaster of Rose Hill, Mr T.G. Hughes, thought it would be best for young new boys to settle into the school two days before all the other boys arrived for the beginning of term. I have clear memories of the early evening of Tuesday, 23 September, when our peace and quiet were rudely shattered by the tremendous noise level, and feeling quite intimidated by the "huge" twelve and thirteen-year-olds. I quickly discovered that there was a school "language" which I had to learn. Prep, PT, elevenses, welsh rarebit, tuck, weakling, blubbing, the cane, bad marks, and many other words and phrases had to be added to my vocabulary. The actual work in form, the three Rs, etc. I found myself to have been very well prepared for by Miss Rutter's kindergarten, and by "Nanny" as governess, and my grandmother at Dunster. I remember, as well as formal lessons, games, "occupations" (i.e. practical work around the school and grounds), etc. some good fun with the other boys during free time, learning card games, writing and guessing games, the sort of games played at children's parties, and so on. One boy had a battery-operated "magic lantern", with all sorts of slides, and it made possible finger shadow displays that provided a lot of fun for many.

Rose Hill School took great care in giving the pupils Christian nurture and teaching. Every morning the whole school attended a short service in the village church (transferred into the school only on the very coldest winter days). On Sundays the school joined villagers for the morning service, and formed by far the greater part of the congregation! I sometimes wondered what it was like in the school holidays – very dead, by comparison, I'm sure. There was one man from the village who always sang extremely loudly, causing some amusement among the boys. It transpired that when the boys weren't there, it was he who kept the hymns going. The school provided a choir, lesson readers and sidesmen from its pupils; and there was a daily rota for pumping the organ. Care was taken in the choice of suitable visiting preachers who would interest and inspire the boys. "Scripture" (so called) was taught with considerable thoroughness in the school. A voluntary Sunday evening hymn-singing session was held in the school about once a month; and just very occasionally evensong took place in the oil-lit church – a really atmospheric event. As Christmas approached the boys were taught a mixture of old and newer carols, culminating in the very popular carol service (some carols sung by the choir, and some by the whole school). Several members of the staff helped me and other boys to grow in our Christian faith and understanding through informal conversations we had with them.

My developing interest in public transport made the rare sight of buses in the village of Alderley rather a thrill for me. The Bristol Tramways Company single-deck buses which passed through the village a few times a day, on Tuesdays, Thursdays, Saturdays and Sundays only, were en route between Wotton-under-Edge and Chipping Sodbury, both quite small towns, which provided shopping facilities for people of nearby villages. Journeys on Mondays, Wednesdays and Fridays passed through different villages on the way between the same termini.

Not many people had cars in the 1940s, and there were great restrictions on their use. So the scarcity of buses meant that the mobility of the villagers was severely limited. I think a good deal of cycling was done – but Rose Hill boys were not allowed to use bicycles. We were expected to be perfectly fit enough to do the two-mile walk to Wotton-under-Edge, and to walk back again, if there was good reason to do so.

The nearest railway stations to Rose Hill were Charfield, on the Gloucester to Bristol section of the then

LMS railway; and Badminton on the GWR line from Paddington to South Wales. The Duke of Beaufort had the right to require any train to stop at Badminton station (which was on his land); he didn't often use that prerogative; but I understand that he did so at the beginning and end of every term for the convenience of Rose Hill School. The majority of boys in the school in the 1940s lived around London and in the Home Counties (remember the school's Surrey origins); and used the train between Paddington and Badminton (a hired bus took them between the station and the school).

Living in Bristol, and with my father unable to use petrol for travelling between our home and the school for most of my time, my brother William and I joined a fairly small number of pupils taken by taxi between the school and Charfield station to and from the Bristol train. I have never forgotten the time of 8.37 a.m., when the train left Charfield for Bristol at the beginning of the holidays; it was a very leisurely stopping train, because it didn't reach Bristol, little over twenty miles' journey, till 9.28 a.m. At the end of my first term, at the age of six, I wasn't really prepared for the holidays.

Our parents were allowed to visit us at school once during the term (though the journey wasn't easy for them when cars could no longer be used). When we went back to Bristol in December 1941, I was a little disorientated at first. Home and school were two completely different worlds. The only link between them for me was my brother William (though the school's policy was always to keep brothers fairly separate from each other during term-time). I rather missed having so much company around me, and home seemed terribly quiet. The structured school day was replaced by a degree of freedom that seemed almost unreal.

Most certainly our parents went to a lot of trouble to keep William and me enjoyably and usefully engaged during the holidays from school. They took us out a good deal to places of interest and amusement in and around Bristol. They encouraged us to read good and educational books. They tried to make sure that we were not "couch potatoes" during the holidays; and certainly the period from about 2.30 to 4 p.m. each day was a time when we were expected to be out of doors. There were good walks from our home over the Downs of Bristol, and on a lot of semi-rural footpaths.

The children of our parents' friends were frequent visitors to our home; we enjoyed indoor and outdoor games with them, and sometimes went to their homes. Our mother held children's parties, and so we got invitations to the parties of those who came. (A bit of a problem came when we were invited to parties where all the other children seemed to know each other from their school, and we felt rather out of it by going to school elsewhere.)

I was very lucky to have William at home in the holidays; there was so much that we could do together, and that increased as we got older, had bicycles, travelled on local buses, could go to the cinema without our parents, and could share toys, games, kits, etc. It was not really until after the war that our parents were able to take us away on holiday. On VJ Day we arrived in Scotland from an overnight train, and got to know relations on our mother's side who lived there. Staying on our uncle and aunt's farm gave us quite a fresh experience. Scottish holidays became a regular feature through much of my schooldays; and in the Easter holidays we generally had a week or so away somewhere in the south or south-west of England. Weston-super-Mare was our "local" seaside resort, very convenient for day-trips and occasionally slightly longer stays.

When I hear of people who were brought up to find Sundays very dull and restrictive, I certainly cannot echo their experience. I think my mother had the idea that if you go to church, then you can do what you like during the rest of Sunday – and that attitude I accepted unquestioningly. Churchgoing fitted into the pattern of the week at home, as it did at school. I daresay that I found some church services that were designed mainly for adults to be a bit dull and lifeless compared with the school services, and it was a case of having to sit through some sermons rather than be enlightened by them. My home church attendance as a prep school boy was mainly at our local parish church; but my father was a sidesman at Bristol Cathedral, where his parents had worshipped regularly – and gradually we went there more often, particularly when I was old enough to appreciate the excellent sermons that were preached there, including those of Canon Leslie Mannering, the founder of the Bible Reading Fellowship.

To go back to Rose Hill School, the school day made

provision for academic lessons in the morning, and from about 5 to 6.30 pm. The earlier part of the afternoon was devoted to sport and outdoor activity. (In the summer term it was the other way round, so that boys would not be exerting themselves physically at the hottest time of the day.) I cannot pretend to have excelled on the sports field; but we were all in it together, and I remember getting keener on football as I concentrated on playing at fullback and tried to do powerful clearances. Hockey was also played a bit, but not rugby football, as I was later to regret (you will see why if you read on). Cricket was the main summer game, with a bit of tennis, and all sorts of informal ball games, wide games, chasing games, etc. became features of summer free time.

In 1942 Cordwalles School, from Camberley, came to Alderley to be temporarily merged with Rose Hill. Another house in the village was acquired, and named "Cordwalles." The Cordwalles boys retained their own uniform; but I think otherwise they completely shared the life of Rose Hillians. Some very capable staff members from Cordwalles enhanced Rose Hill life. I had expected to go with Rose Hill back to Banstead at the end of the war; and my parents had plans that my brother William should go to Camberley with Cordwalles when it returned, because he seemed to get on particularly well with the Cordwalles headmaster and other staff and boys.

However, things didn't work out like that, because the Rose Hill authorities decided not to go back to Banstead at all. Rose Hill had very good amenities in such lovely Cotswold countryside, and so it stayed put, and is still there, though now co-educational. (Actually there were a very few girls for a time in Rose Hill when I was there, but their parents must have felt quite happy for them to be so vastly outnumbered by boys!) When Cordwalles went back to Camberley, a few Cordwalles staff stayed on at Rose Hill; and our parents thought that in the circumstances William and I might just as well both remain at Rose Hill. I should add that I think the pupils were extremely well looked after, cared for, dare I say loved, by the teaching staff and matrons at Rose Hill; and the food was remarkably good, in view of the wartime and post-war rationing.

CHAPTER 3

Bicycles, the Latest modern post-war buses, the old steam trains again, and more Daimlers.

At the age of thirteen I was sent by my parents to Marlborough College, where my father had been a pupil. The day I started there, he said to me, "I'm glad it's you going, not me!" There seemed to be a widespread idea that Marlborough was a very tough school – but by the late 1940s that was not really true or fair. People on hearing that I was to go there said to my father, "So you really want to toughen Henry up!" The system by which all new boys started in a Junior House was meant to ease the transition from prep school to public school. I would not dispute that there was a certain amount of bullying at Marlborough; but there were common sense ways of reducing the likelihood of becoming a victim of it. Right from the start at Marlborough I met some boys whom I liked very much, and I think one found one's own level fairly quickly.

I mentioned in the last chapter my regret that I had not been taught to play rugby football at Rose Hill. I soon discovered that just about everyone else was reasonably familiar with the game. New boys were pitchforked into "trial" games of rugby (or "rugger" as it was always called); maybe my father should have made sure that I knew at any rate the rudiments of the game, but he expected that it would be taught from scratch. My ignorance and ineptness annoyed some on my side in the early trial games, and not surprisingly I was put into the lowest, the "third", standard. I must say that I had not realised that "rugger" would be quite so rough as it turned out to be. Intensive practices and "friendly" games were held to get the "thirds" up to scratch; and it was regarded as extremely important that every boy should play rugger to his full potential. I could not quite see why it was thought to be so vital as all that. I can't say that I ever really enjoyed rugger – but that's just me. Many boys loved it.

Soccer was not played much; but on the rare occasions when we did play it was regarded as more of a relaxation. Hockey was the main sport for the January term; and it never seemed to be taken nearly as seriously as rugger, or certainly not at the lower levels. Everyone had to play cricket in the summer term, at any rate for their first few years. I preferred to be "scorer" when possible; and my willingness to do so seemed to be appreciated, as it was not a very popular job!

The college chapel at Marlborough played an important part in school life. Every morning a twenty-minute service was compulsory, and the singing raised the roof. The noise took a bit of getting used to for new boys. On Sundays there was an hour-long service in the morning which all had to attend. Sometimes one of the chaplains or the "Master" (i.e. the headmaster) would preach. On other Sundays there would be visiting preachers, mainly chosen from those who were well-known as being good with schoolboys. The Revd C.J. Ellingham, from Kent, evidently did the rounds of the public schools and when he came, he always had everyone in fits of laughter. Occasionally a Bishop would come, not because he was particularly good at addressing teenagers, but because he was a Bishop. Re-reading a diary I kept, I found that I described a certain Bishop's sermon as "dull". That really set me thinking. "What would the Master have said to him after the service? If he made such a poor impression on a future ordinand, what was that bishop really trying to do? What did he think the boys would gain from his sermon? Or was it my fault that communication had failed?"

Compulsory chapel was, I think, generally accepted as part of school discipline. A few boys noticeably took no active part in the worship, giving the impression that they were just there on sufferance. However, in addition to services that everyone had to attend, there were voluntary services also, notably a devotional service on Thursday evenings, which was quite well attended. There was early Holy Communion on Sundays, when many boys received the sacrament, and on some weekdays. I was Confirmed at Marlborough, and gained much from the preparation that the chaplain gave. Confirmation was not "automatic"; you had to take the initiative to enrol for classes – I would think that well over half the boys did. The chaplains got in touch with the vicars of the parishes where the boys who were Confirmed lived. I remember joining in and enjoying religious discussion groups after Confirmation. After prep each night there were "house prayers". "Scripture" was taught as part of the curriculum for everyone.

A major feature of life at Marlborough when I was there was the Corps. Everyone in their second year had to join the Army section; and after getting through "Certificate A" had the option of transferring to the Naval, Air Force or Signals sections of the Combined Cadet Force if they wished. I stayed in the Army section, anticipating call-up for National Service; and most certainly it was a great advantage to have had training in the CCF when you joined the "real" army. A summer camp was part of the training we received. Of course being in the Corps meant wearing uniform and boots, which were subject to rigorous inspection. A few "cadet NCOs" seemed to relish bring thoroughly beastly to younger boys whose "turn-out" they found fault with. It gave them a feeling of power, and maybe it was their way of handling their own inferiority complexes.

Marlborough had a station on the cross-country "Andover to Andoversford" railway line, part of British Railways when I knew it, and it was particularly useful to many in providing connections at Savernake (12 minutes away) with express trains to London. A special through train for the school ran between Paddington and Marlborough at the beginning and end of every term. When I went home to Bristol, I went westwards from Savernake, either on a through train, or with a change at Westbury, Wilts. It was also possible to travel between Bristol and Marlborough on the precursor of National Express, the coach service operated from Bristol to London jointly by "Greyhound" (Bristol Tramways Co.) and "Royal Blue" (Western National). I used that once or twice at the beginning of term, if my father could not take me by car.

It was before the days of the M4, and the coaches stopped in the very wide High Street, a famous feature of Marlborough. There were also north-south coaches via Marlborough, which were part of the "Associated Motorways" network which provided a huge range of possible connections at Cheltenham Coach Station. We often saw "Black and White" coaches on this network calling at Marlborough en route between Cheltenham and Portsmouth. Marlborough was served by regular buses of a more local nature. The Bristol Tramways Company had an hourly double-decked route from Swindon, going on beyond Marlborough to Savernake Hospital. Single-decker Bristol buses ran from Marlborough to Calne and to Hungerford via Ramsbury. Sometimes I saw buses which I remembered having seen or travelled in at Bristol. The Wilts. and Dorset Company ran its red double-deckers to Salisbury from Marlborough by two routes, one every hour via Pewsey and Amesbury, and the other every two hours via Tidworth. Wilts. and Dorset also provided some Saturday market day services from villages south of Marlborough. The long inter-urban bus services were very reliable, but extremely slow, taking, for instance, an hour and a half to reach Salisbury by the quicker route. At places they left the main roads to serve villages. While I was at Marlborough I saw the pre-war buses gradually being replaced by new ones. Wilts. and Dorset had new Bristol type double-deckers in place of old Leyland Titans. Even the new ones, I'm pretty sure, only had five-cylinder engines; so they laboured a bit on the rural hills. The Bristol Company tended to use pre-war double-deckers on the Swindon route, with smart new bodies, making them look like new buses – but the time-tables were geared to their sluggish performance!

Actually I got around a good deal from Marlborough on my bicycle, with trips to Salisbury and Stonehenge, Bath, Cirencester and Chedworth Roman Villa, Malmesbury, Lechlade for boating on the Thames, and a number of other places. On some days, after exams, we were encouraged to go "outward bound" – bikes in those days were not multi-geared as now, just having three gears to use; and I am sure those long cycle rides increased my fitness enormously. The prospect of National Service concentrated one's mind on the absolute necessity of being in the best possible physical condition for the demands that the Army would make.

The holidays from Marlborough became for William and me more and more a matter of doing what we wanted to do unsupervised by our parents. (Incidentally, William went to Marlborough two years after I started there, but we were in different houses, and didn't see all that much of each other.) One thing we took up in the holidays was Croquet (I mean proper Association Croquet) at the Bristol club, where our father was chairman. He subsequently wrote the first edition of *Know the Game; Croquet*; and William in a few years was playing for England. I found it, and still do, a fascinating game. In the winter holidays we were invited to a considerable number of private dances in Bristol; it was "de rigueur" to be able to do the various steps, including eightsome reels, etc., and some square dancing – so our mother arranged for us to attend dancing classes for several years. It did mean that we met girls, and that was important for those at an all-boys school. We had quite a social programme with Bristol friends; but the one thing I couldn't bear was going beagling on Boxing Day. The prospect spoilt Christmas. And seeing a girl gleefully displaying a hare's blood all over her face made me quite sick!

I took great interest in the replacement of the buses that had originally replaced Bristol's trams by new and more powerful, and wider and more comfortable, Bristol-type double-deckers. While both the new and the old buses were operating on the same routes to the same schedules, the old ones had difficulty in keeping up with the new ones, particularly on Bristol's steep hills. The new buses took the hills in their stride, even when fully loaded; while the old ones got down to not much more than walking speed in their very low first gear – but they always seemed to make it to the top! I was also fascinated by time-table changes and route extensions as Bristol spread further out. From observation from our window, I could plot the times when a particular bus would pass our house for the rest of the day. Was that a good use of mental effort? As you will see, it certainly proved to be so, in a very unexpected way.

Our parents took us on some lovely holidays during Marlborough years. Our first trip abroad was through

France in my father's Daimler, landing up at Biarritz for a week, and visiting Paris on the way back. Scottish holidays tended now to be by car, rather than train, taking rather roundabout routes (e.g. via Cambridge), and so seeing many places where I had never been before. Oban was a favourite destination of my parents. From there we visited my aunt staying on Iona; and as soon as we got off the boat the first person I met was a boy with whom I had been at Rose Hill.

When I moved from my junior house, Barton Hill, to a senior house, Cotton House, I got a study, which I shared with a boy called David Nobbs. If that name seems familiar, remember Reginald Perrin. David was later to be the creator of that well-known character. The books were dramatised on television. David wrote quite a number of novels, and has published his autobiography, *I Didn't Get Where I Am To-day*. I found David to be excellent company. We shared rather the same kind of humour. He was a great deflater of pomposity. David and I learned a lot from each other about each other's family background, and we stayed in each other's homes a bit during the holidays. He almost became like another brother to me. There were a number of other boys in Cotton House and other houses whom I found very congenial; and I do remember there being a very good spirit, particularly during the latter part of my time.

Our housemaster, Mr E.H. Dowdell, a mathematician, was unobtrusive, but he knew what was going on. His fanaticism for rugger disconcerted me a bit; he told me to make sure I joined in informal practices with other boys on days when I wasn't playing in a game or match. There was a plentiful supply of rugby balls to be borrowed for an afternoon; Mr. Dowdell knew who did and who didn't use them! He was a caring man, and approachable; he expected all to give of their best in everything, and if you gave him reason to think you were doing that, you had nothing to fear from him.

I haven't yet mentioned the academic side of life at Marlborough, which you may say was our main reason for being there. We had to work for O-levels and A-levels and a large proportion of boys aspired to going on to university. It may seem strange – but when I think back to Marlborough days, other features of life there seem more vivid in my memory than sitting down at desks, and being taught, and getting on with work. I joined the Classical side, studying Latin, Greek and Ancient History to A-level standard; and I remember some inspiring teachers. It is better, I think, not to mention their names, for fear of leaving out any to whom I owed a debt. When I left I had been offered a place at Pembroke College, Cambridge, to read Classics, with the proviso that I completed National Service first. More of that in the next chapter.

CHAPTER 4

Troop Carriers, My Own Two Feet in Boots, more Steam Trains, "Express" 30 mph Coaches, and a Sea Voyage.

Everyone of the male sex had to register for National Service, on pain of severe threatened penalties; and in due course there came the summons to a medical examination for that purpose. Then, provided that you had been accepted as medically fit and with a suitable physique for the armed services, there came a time of waiting to be called up. My uncle, who owned a day prep-school for boys just outside London, invited me to spend a bit of that waiting time at his school – obviously not giving me responsibilities for which I was not fitted or trained, but being a classroom assistant, taking groups of boys on their own, standing in if a teacher was ill with clear instructions of what we were supposed to be doing, giving a bit of secretarial and administrative help, and taking 8 to 9-year-olds for football.

It concerned me that one or two boys took absolutely no part in the game, never kicked the ball once. When I tried to get them more involved, they melted into tears. I wondered what their parents expected of the school regarding their sons' physical education, and what encouragement they gave them in the holidays to play in a park with friends. If my call-up papers came, I could easily leave the school in mid-term. As it was, after the term ended I got a summons to report for duty at the Royal Artillery Camp at Park Hall, just outside Oswestry, Shropshire. It was not a part of the country that I knew at all.

I remember the train journey on my call-up day very well, feeling apprehensive, naturally; and I had been a bit alarmed by stories I had heard about how recruits were treated at some Army units. At Oswestry station we were treated to a ride in a Crosville double-decker bus to the camp; I had expected a cramped and uncomfortable troop-carrying lorry. I remember getting off the bus, and looking round, and thinking, "So this is it", when a sergeant quickly took us in hand and marched us quickly to our various barrack-rooms.

That first afternoon was taken up with documentation, getting fitted out with uniform and equipment, and trying to get into one's kit-bag far more stuff than it seemed to be able to accommodate. I remember the huge piles of boots, from which we had to extract ones that were our size – and a helpful "quartermaster" saying, "Don't be afraid to take brown boots. Of course you'll have to dye them black – but they're the best, the strongest and the most comfortable boots that soldiers have ever had." I did not regret taking his advice, and when my two pairs of brown boots were gleaming black, I did not suffer the discomfort that some had who had taken the older type of black boots.

A thing that I came very quickly to notice was the high noise level everywhere; and I realised that it was of course the effect of everyone clattering around in their boots. No rubber soles in those days, but steel-rimmed heels, and hobnails on the soles. An officer giving us a pep-talk said a soldier's boots are his most precious possessions; look after them, and they'll look after you. As is well-known that "looking-after" required polishing to a tremendously high degree of shine; it was regarded as a proper cause for pride to be seen in boots that glinted in the sunlight.

To be fair, while conditions were certainly tough for recruits at Park Hall, I don't think the awful sort of stories of cruelty that I had heard had their counterparts where we were. A few young NCOs may have abused their authority a bit – but you just had to let foul language go in at one ear and out at the other. Those who were really physically fit had a great advantage over those who had neglected that aspect of preparation for National Service. Certainly some found the physical demands utterly exhausting. Those who had been at boarding school, or had spent a good deal of time away from home, were better able, on the whole, to cope with the sudden and complete separation from their families.

Those whose mothers had done everything for them were left floundering when they had to look after themselves, their clothes and all their equipment. Wise preparation for National Service most certainly included gaining familiarity with the use of various cleaning materials, elementary sewing, and ensuring competence at such jobs as lighting fires (without firelighters), and chopping wood. (Incidentally, when ordered to smash up large pieces of wood to provide kindling wood for fires, and finding no tools, we were told, "You don't need tools. Use your boots!" That, I'm sure, was all part of the Army's way of trying to make young soldiers stronger and fitter – and thankful to be wearing boots, not ordinary shoes!) Drill played an important part in basic training; and we were soon introduced to specific features of the Royal Artillery.

I was selected for training as Technical Assistant, for which the main qualification was mathematics at O-level. That training included the gun drill which all Artillery members had to get competent in. We went to fire the big guns in a wild expanse of Wales, some travelling in the discomfort of troop-carrying lorries, some in the comparative comfort of Crosville buses. The buses were better hill-climbers than the lorries!

Barrack-room life completely took away all social distinctions. There was a real corporate sense of being all in it together. Those who had difficulties of one sort or another were supported by their comrades. A few who were rather cocky and boastful caused some annoyance; but I think they were generally put in their place by the clear disapproval of their attitudes. I do know of one or two who found it all too much, and the continuing noise of crashing boots everywhere got on their nerves. We never knew of what happened to the very small number who "disappeared".

The spiritual side of life was officially under the care of the military chaplains. On certain Sundays there were compulsory church parades for all except Roman Catholics, who had their own arrangements. I felt the emphasis was on "parade" rather than "church." I mustn't be unfair, but it did seem to me that the chaplains could and should have made the services (in the camp cinema) rather more suitable for young men with little or no church connections. The services were not on the whole well received, though one chaplain was a bit of a comedian. I didn't like singing in that setting "Onward, Christian soldiers" anything like as much as I did at Dunster, and still less "From Greenland's icy mountains", with its Victorian smugness, quite out of place at a compulsory church parade, where there were many with a fragile, searching or virtually non-existent faith.

Similarly the "padre's hour" was rather a lost opportunity; one chaplain tried to address and hold the interest of far too many soldiers; and quite a number regarded that hour as literally a time to catch up with lost sleep. There were voluntary Holy Communion services but few attended them out of the very large number of men in the camp. Quite a different religious dimension came with visiting evangelists, who went round barrackrooms distributing tracts, and rather getting people's backs up by their "hard-sell" of Christianity. I had never experienced anything like that before, and wondered what the chaplains thought. The evangelists seemed rather dismissive of the more "official" Christian worship and teaching that were under the chaplains' control, a situation not very unlike what I was later to find at university! A group of us sometimes went to evensong at a church in Oswestry, and in fact a fair proportion of the congregation was in Artillery uniform.

Transport-wise, Park Hall Camp had two railway stations, on two different local lines, within short walking distance. Some parts of the camp were nearer one (Park Hall Halt) and some nearer the other (Tinkers Green Halt). From neither of them were trains into Oswestry very frequent; but they could save a walk if you went at the right time. The main ex-Great Western express route from Paddington to Birkenhead passed very close to the camp, and access to it was at Gobowen, from where a branch went to Park Hall and Oswestry.

I think the large Artillery camp was responsible for Gobowen having as good a service as it did. For Bristol I changed from the London line at Shrewsbury. Oswestry's local buses belonged to the very extensive Crosville company. Newer ones were of the Bristol type. Regular services extended to Wrexham, Welshpool and villages for which Oswestry served as a shopping centre. Though Oswestry is in England, it is very near the Welsh border, and certainly in 1953 seemed to have rather a Welsh atmosphere about it. I thought it a pleasant town. The local inhabitants may have thought it was a bit too much overrun by soldiers!

The question arose as to whether I should apply for selection for officer training. Actually, I did attend the War Office Selection Board residential conference near Andover, Hants (a change of scene from Shropshire). I was not accepted for officer training, a right decision, I'm sure – I could hardly see myself at that young age as at all suitable to join in life in the mess, let alone inspect and order soldiers about. Some of my friends had become

National Service officers – but I think they had rather different qualities and personalities from me. Nevertheless, my visit to WOSB, as it was known, did have very big repercussions, because, at the suggestion of the chief interviewing officer, I left the Artillery, and joined the Intelligence Corps. I was told to expect a posting soon; and one day at 5 p.m. at Oswestry I was suddenly told that I must catch a train at 8 a.m. the following day to go to the Intelligence Corps Depot at Maresfield, near Uckfield, Sussex. I hastily had to get all my kit ready to take, in FSMO (full service marching order), and would have liked a bit more notice before a quick "goodbye" to my Artillery friends.

At Maresfield we were put through various assessments before they decided into which branch of the Intelligence Corps to put us; there was a fairly general corps training first, interspersed with a good deal of "square-bashing", weapons training, etc. There were some tough drill parades. No one was meant to think that the Intelligence Corps was a "cushy" posting. Boots still had to be polished immaculately! Of course everyone there had been sent because they were thought to be potentially suitable – and so it was perhaps more like a university than a typical army camp as far as one's fellow-trainees were concerned. I was led to expect to do the "Field Security" course. However, I found myself summoned to an interview for MI8 (top secret work). You could only be selected – you couldn't apply – for that; and screening and vetting processes were pretty thorough. Among the questions asked me by the interviewer was, "Do you collect train numbers?" I explained that that was the sort of thing that interested me, but that we did not live close enough to a railway line to be able to do it very conveniently – however, I did collect bus numbers and at that his face lit up.

For reasons better known to himself at that time than to me, that interest of mine seemed to be just the sort of thing he was looking for in prospective MI8 staff. When I did the training course, I soon came to see the connection! But I'm still bound by the Official Secrets Act, and can't divulge more. Actually, I had to go to Gloucester for the MI8 training; and though there remained the possibility that afterwards I might be sent abroad, in actual fact I spent the rest of my National Service as a member of the military staff at GCHQ, Cheltenham. There we worked in civilian clothes – but I had to keep my uniform and boots up to scratch for occasional training days and special parades; we mustn't forget that we were in the army. I lived in rooms in Cheltenham, and kept up with my landlady for some time afterwards; she and her husband visited us at Bristol; I understood that the landladies were specially vetted, and there were strict rules about complete secrecy when we were off GCHQ premises.

At Maresfield the rather elderly vicar of the village church acted as chaplain to the Intelligence Corps camp. He was a real sport; and seemed to enjoy the quite heated religious arguments that developed during the padre's hour. A number of us attended the village church regularly on Sundays. A midweek service was held in the camp; occasionally it was compulsory, but on the occasions when it was voluntary there was good attendance. A variety of preachers came, and care was obviously taken in the choice of them, bearing in mind the type of audience they had! At Cheltenham there was no specific religious provision for the soldiers disguised in mufti. Most weekends I went home to Bristol; if I was at Cheltenham I attended a local church.

I will add a bit about transport in the places where I served with the Intelligence Corps. The nearest railway station to Maresfield was Uckfield, about three miles away. It was then served by Southern Region steam trains to Victoria. It was generally thought to be quicker to go to Haywards Heath on the hourly Uckfield to Horsham Southdown bus, which passed the camp, and then board one of the fast and frequent electric trains to London. For weekend leave privately hired Southdown coaches ran from the camp to Victoria Coach Station in London; they returned at 10 p.m. on Sunday nights. Maresfield, like most of Sussex, was extremely well served by buses of the Southdown empire. The Brighton to Tunbridge Wells (joint Southdown and Maidstone & District) and the Eastbourne to East Grinstead services passed through Maresfield hourly; also there were some more local routes. It was said that conductors did not like being rostered for the last bus back from Brighton on Saturday nights; and usually a hefty inspector travelled on that journey! Southdown had a mainly double-deck fleet for their long inter-urban routes. Some were the latest Leyland Titans. Some were pre-war ones that had recently been rebodied. Gloucester, the scene of the MI8 course at the "Gloucesters" depot was in the Bristol Tramways Company's extensive operating area.

The city routes, rather like Bristol's, were run by the company with financial and planning responsibilities shared with the city corporation. The Bristol-type double-deckers carried the Gloucester city coat of arms. At Cheltenham I travelled to work each day in "Cheltenham District" red buses. This all-double-deck fleet was under the control of Bristol Tramways by then, and ran a good service, with a mixture of new Bristol-type buses, and older Guys, Albions and AEC's. When at Cheltenham I sampled many country bus routes from the town, to places in the Cotswolds, to Malvern, Tewkesbury, Cirencester, Stroud, Evesham, etc. Cheltenham was rather a boundary town between Bristol Tramways, Midland Red, Stratford Blue, and Pulhams and Marchants, who served the north-east Cotswolds (Stow-on-the-Wold, etc.), an area that none of the big bus operators had colonised.

The Bristol company also worked a through route to Bristol, via Gloucester, every hour. If I went home it was a good deal quicker to get the express trains on the Birmingham to Bristol line; but I did occasionally take the double-decker bus, with its leisurely schedule – and once or twice the Associated Motorways coach, bound for Paignton, via Bristol, from Cheltenham's up-market coach station.

The day came when my two years' National Service was up, and so my next thing was to take up my place at

Pembroke College, Cambridge, with memories of a lot of fun and friendship at Cheltenham, and stimulating work. We had had close association with the civilian staff, with one of whom I regained contact forty-six years later; she attended the service at Horley, near Banbury, when I celebrated the fortieth anniversary of my Ordination, as she was living fairly close nearby; and seeing a mention of that forthcoming service in the local newspaper, she put two and two together from distant memories, thinking there would not be more than one Henry Ormerod, of about the most likely age. It was lovely to see her again.

My Latin and Greek were a bit rusty by the time I had finished National Service; and my Cambridge tutor gave me a programme of study to undertake before the Cambridge term began in October, 1955. I know a lot of people had boring jobs during their National Service, once their intensive early training was finished – so I counted myself lucky. Attendance at Army Reserve camp was required the following year. I spent a wet fortnight under canvas on the edge of the North York Moors, and was continually having to clean my mud-spattered boots for morning parade and inspection! I was not called up for reservists' training after that.

To begin with at Cambridge, I found it difficult to adjust to the very great degree of freedom that there was, compared with everywhere I had been before, except for home. Planning one's own work required much care and self-discipline. I met up with lots of people I had known at school (Rose Hill as well as Marlborough), a few from Army days, and others whom I knew from Bristol social life.

One's memories of university are often said to be largely memories of good friends. Among a number of people whom I liked very much at Pembroke College was Robert Philp (reading Classics, and then staying on to do research). He was to have a long and much valued career on the teaching staff at Fettes College, Edinburgh; in fact he wrote the official history of that college, *A Keen Wind Blows*. I have kept up with him ever since Cambridge days, and he is godfather to our daughter Sarah. I felt Robert and I had a lot in common in our outlook on life and in our approach to the Christian Faith; his integrity, his caring personality, and his utterly sincere charm impressed me very much, and gave me some standards to aspire to. A godmother of Sarah is Margaret Edmonds (née Jordan), whom I got to know and like through the Student Christian Movement. She was at Hughes Hall graduate teacher training college in Cambridge, and she invited me to tea in her room there on Sunday, 24 November, 1957.

It was at that tea party that I first met another Hughes Hall student, Priscilla Mallinson. No wonder I like to remember the anniversary of that day – for Priscilla is now, and has been for a long time, Priscilla Ormerod. Priscilla and I now have three grown-up children and four grandchildren.

I mentioned earlier the barrack-room evangelists at Oswestry and I found something on rather similar lines at Cambridge. Our college, and every college, had a group of very "heart-on-sleeve Christians", who were keen that freshmen (i.e. new undergraduates) should have the opportunity of hearing the Christian Gospel, and making their own personal response of faith in Christ. Since Oswestry days I had come to hear of Billy Graham's missions, and realised that they were on the same wavelength as him – and indeed Billy Graham himself was coming to conduct a mission at Cambridge that very term. These initiatives were under the auspices of CICCU (Cambridge Inter-Collegiate Christian Union). I attended some services and meetings in response to CICCU invitations – but felt that I was breathing a different air from all my previous experience of church membership.

At one large tea party addressed by a future evangelical bishop of the Church of England, when a lot was said about linking up with the "right" churches, I ventured to mention the college chapels as the natural spiritual homes of undergraduates. I was a bit puzzled by the way that intervention was received, with a certain amount of laughter, and, "Yes, but...". Clearly some college chapels didn't quite suit the CICCU! Anyhow, that was all part of my spiritual education. The Dean of Chapel of my college assured me that the breadth of the Church of England was part of its strength. I did go to Billy Graham, did publicly profess faith in Christ in response to his appeal; and I was subsequently put in touch with a small group of undergraduates who would "help me on". It would be wrong to say that I did not gain some valuable spiritual insights from all this – but it was very different from my earlier Christian nurture that had meant so much to me.

I was puzzled and alarmed too by the "fundamentalist" approach to Scripture and Salvation that I encountered, that seemed to fly in the face of what I thought were generally accepted scholarly conclusions about the make-up of the Bible. Efforts were made to try to get me to take part in a beach mission in Norfolk. After a lot of thought and perusal of the literature, I really felt that this wasn't for me. Opportunities opened up to meet with other Christians through the Student Christian Movement (SCM); and I must say that my faith there was very much more stimulated; they seemed to speak much more the same language as myself about spiritual matters. Let alone the indirect result of meeting Priscilla!

Pembroke College Chapel was the heart of a closely-knit worshipping community, on weekdays as well as Sundays. The Dean, whom I have already mentioned, The Revd M.B. Dewey I came to know very well. I can certainly say that he was instrumental in encouraging and helping me forward towards Ordination. After four terms at Cambridge I attended the Church of England selection conference for prospective ordinands. That itself was a stimulating and learning experience. Some tough questions were asked, but in an atmosphere of prayer and of real Christian charity. No one was trying to score points over anyone else. I soon learned that the panel had recommended me for training towards Ordination. The Bristol Diocese Director of Ordination Candidates (Canon John Peacey) was very helpful indeed to me. From his knowledge of Theological Training Colleges, he thought The Queen's College, Birmingham, would be very suitable for me – as it most certainly turned out to be. I visited the college, and the Principal, Canon Arthur Gribble, offered me a place there when I had completed my Cambridge course.

It seemed to make sense, too, that instead of sticking with Classics at Cambridge, I should transfer to Theology for my last year in the university. It was a bit tough to do virtually two years' work in one by making the change – however, I did better in theology than I had done in the first part of the Classics tripos, and am sure that my future ministry owed a lot to the very stimulating theological course, with lectures by the future bishop John Robinson, by Professor Charlie Moule (who somehow managed to make his lectures something of a devotional experience) and others from whom I gained a lot.

You can probably guess that I was not into "main-line" sport at Cambridge – my standards had never been up to joining in with people at university level who had opted for sports that they had earlier excelled at or enjoyed greatly. However, my brother William (who also joined Pembroke College) and I did have a lot to do with putting association croquet much more on the map. We both played for a university team at that sport in the summer – but no blues, half-blues or even quarter-blues were on offer!

Going to Cambridge opened up for me a new transport scene. The railways were beginning to change over from steam traction to diesel; and the more local lines started to be served by the new type of diesel multiple unit trains. It was possible to sit behind the driver, and get the same view as he had of the line ahead. I found that quite fascinating. Cambridge railway station was, and is, quite a way from the city centre (originally the university wanted the railway well out of the way). The beneficiary of that was the Cambridge city bus system; at the time when I was there this was under the control of Eastern Counties Omnibus Company, which had widespread services throughout East Anglia. Bristol-type buses were largely used; five-cylinder engines were standard, and thought to be quite adequate for the flat territory in which the buses operated.

More than in other places where I had been, the Saturday bus services tended to be enhanced, to meet the demands arising from the East Anglian custom of going out on Saturdays. This was before car ownership had really taken off. I suppose that the extra Saturday buses were those that during the week operated school and works services. Sundays also still saw pretty good bus services in town and country. Most undergraduates probably seldom had reason to use local buses in and around Cambridge – but I sometimes explored the area a bit by bus and partly by train, as well as occasionally by bicycle.

Our holidays in the 1950s often included taking part in croquet tournaments in various parts of the country. Croquet clubs tended to be in "desirable" areas; and I have memories of tournaments at Eastbourne, Southwick (near Brighton), Parkstone (near Bournemouth), Leamington Spa, Nottingham University, Cheltenham, Hunstanton, Norfolk, Budleigh Salterton, Devon, and the

Roehampton and Hurlingham Clubs in London. I also did "extended" bus trips, using a succession of ordinary service buses (not express coaches) to tour parts of the country. My longest such trip was to Scotland, to stay with relations there, and back via a different route.

I really got to know the bus network, which was much more comprehensive than many people realised. Sometimes I used "express" coaches – which were not really very express at all, because they were limited to a speed of thirty miles an hour. It was possible to travel between Cambridge and Bristol by coach, using the Associated Motorways Cheltenham interchange; I enjoyed doing that a few times. Another time I went by service buses from Cambridge, changing at Bedford, Aylesbury, and High Wycombe (United Counties and Thames Valley companies), to board the Bristol train at Reading.

Whenever I used buses for longer distance journeys, nothing ever went wrong or certainly not of any serious nature. Once the driver of an Aldershot and District bus that I was on sounded his horn, but the horn would not stop sounding when he released the button; so we were delayed at Alton, en route from Farnham to Winchester for twenty minutes or so till that awful sound could be stopped! Once or twice I travelled in buses that were not in the best of mechanical health; but they managed to complete their journeys, even if the driver had rather a difficult time with repeated stalling, or gearbox or clutch trouble.

In 1957, my parents' Silver Wedding year, they took William and me on a cruise, because they themselves had originally met on a cruise. We boarded the P&O liner *Chusan* at Southampton, and spent eight days on her, calling at Lisbon and Madeira. The first night the sea got quite rough, and people were having difficulty in dancing without falling over! My father, who was feeling absolutely dreadful, while people were being seasick all over the place, said, "Oh dear! We spend all that money, and then have to put up with this!" Fortunately, conditions never got anything like as bad as that again.

On that British ship we felt we were in England; and at the ports of call we were undoubtedly abroad; changing from one to the other, and changing back again, was rather a funny experience. We made an unscheduled call at the island of Porto Santo, because some stowaways had been found to have boarded at nearby Madeira; and they had to be disembarked. The custom was – I don't know whether it still is – to have a religious service, led by the ship's captain, on Sunday mornings. I remember a hymn we had, "Summer suns are glowing over land and sea" (an obvious one, I suppose, for a summer cruise), and being quite surprised by how well most people seemed to know that hymn and its evocative tune "Ruth" – I didn't think I had ever sung it before. Now I always think of that cruise when I hear it – as I also think back to attending the English church in Bordeaux on our way to Biarritz in 1950 when I hear the Easter hymn, "Come, ye faithful, raise the strain of triumphant gladness". I had never known that hymn until singing it for the first time there, and thinking how lovely it was. (Though I was once asked whether its line "Loosed from Pharaoh's bitter yoke" meant that Pharaoh had a bad egg at Easter!) On the cruise my brother and I seemed to spend a lot of time playing table tennis in a tournament among the guests; I don't think we actually won it; but we got through a number of rounds playing doubles together.

During all the time when we were on the cruise, and for a short period afterwards, there was a national bus strike in England. London was not affected (though it did have its own prolonged strike the following year), and I don't think municipally owned transport joined the strike either; but across enormous swathes of the country there were no buses at all. For those interested in the social history of transport, the 1957 strike was really something of a watershed. There was a tradition that bus travel was cheap for passengers – but that cheapness was on the backs of the bus crews. At that time bus workers' wages compared unfavourably with those in many industries. Much better paid driving jobs were available.

A crisis was developing in the provision of public transport. Bus operators were having real difficulty in attracting and retaining staff. It had to be time for the public to realise that bus travel could no longer be cheap, and the public perception was gradually changed into thinking of bus travel as expensive. Of course, the fact that more and more cars were coming on to the roads meant that there were fewer passengers on the buses; services were then cut, particularly in the evenings and at weekends, when car owners could take their families to places of entertainment, for social visits, for Saturday shopping, etc. Television was keeping people at home in the evenings too.

The economics of running bus services had got very difficult. For some time after the provincial and London strikes of 1957 and 1958, there were pockets of industrial unrest on the nation's bus services. Local repeated strikes on, say, one day of the week were becoming all too common, and putting people off bus travel. Bus crews' pay was taking a long time to catch up with that of people with comparable responsibilities elsewhere. Staff shortages continued in many places; and when that led to random cancellations of scheduled journeys without notice, the public began seriously to lose confidence in their local bus service – many wouldn't dare to try to use buses if they had important appointments to keep or trains to connect with.

Traffic congestion was also beginning to play havoc with bus timetables. I will say a bit more later about developments in south-east Essex in 1967 that I witnessed at first hand, and that caused no end of public outrage. However, I do think lessons were learnt by the management, and some changes in policy did lead to a more stable and reliable set-up. By the late 1950s, many buses were losing their conductors. On lighter routes it was felt that the driver could satisfactorily collect fares; and those drivers who opted to do so got a bit more pay.

The next two decades or so saw single manning become the norm, helped by modern developments in technology. After leaving Cambridge University, and before starting at The Queen's Theological College, Birmingham, I worked for a time in the enquiries' office of what was by then called the Bristol Omnibus

Company (no longer Tramways!). I learned a lot, not least about morale or lack of it among those who were trying to provide satisfactory public transport for the citizens of Bristol and for people in the large part of the "mid-west" which the company served.

What a gulf there seemed to be between those members of society who had the freedom they perceived as going with possession of their own private transport, and those who were dependent on the way Bristol Omnibus Co. handled its monopoly position as transport provider for those without their own wheels. It interested me to see how people knew the bus services that passed their home, travelling frequently on the same journey; but when it came to wanting to go anywhere else by bus, they were completely flummoxed, and nervous about leaving familiar routes for the unfamiliar.

My two years at "Queen's" in Edgbaston, Birmingham, led up to my Ordination as Deacon, and after a further year I was ordained Priest, in the Church of England. I liked Queen's and my fellow-students there, and the principal, Canon Gribble, and other staff. The course was designed to prepare us for the various aspects of the life and work of a clergyman, with considerable emphasis on the devotional side, which should rightly undergird everything. The college chapel was the heart of the community's life. I always felt somehow that a strength of Queen's was that it was not identified too much with any "party" in the Church of England. We learned from the insights and experience of fellow-students whose churchmanship was a bit different from our own. Some Theological Colleges seemed to cater only for ordinands of a particular brand of church tradition, Anglo-Catholic, Evangelical, or Liberal. I had never thought of myself as being "labelled" in such a way, or as belonging to a specific "party" within the Church of England.

Apart from the specifically "theological" teaching and devotional practice, the college tried to help its members to face the realities of what they would find in the parishes where they would go to be curates. Some very good lectures and seminars on social studies were held weekly, with visiting speakers who had knowledge and expertise in various fields, such as work with young people, including teenagers who had got into trouble, or in health services, voluntary welfare organisations, local authorities, factories, and so on. Visits were sometimes arranged to follow on from lectures.

There was also at that time an expectation that young curates would be involved with youth clubs in parishes. The college provided facilities for polishing up our skills at table tennis and snooker, for we would probably find ourselves playing such games with the young people of our parishes! Also, many churches had their own football and cricket teams; and curates who could acquit themselves reasonably well at those sports might have advantages! Opportunities were given at college for those who wished to play cricket and football to do so. "Friendly" matches against various college and community teams were arranged. Those in the college who were good players "carried" the others to some extent. Surprisingly, perhaps, we had some field hockey matches too; and I found myself in goal, where the rules allowed use of feet as well as hockey stick. Cricket pads and my rugby boots from school days were regarded as adequate protective equipment for defending the goal from the onslaughts of the hard hockey ball! At cricket I went back to my old job as scorer; and on at least one occasion at football I was linesman.

The two-year course at Queen's contained much practical training as well as book learning. A number of us, including myself, took the Diploma in Theology at Birmingham university, thereby getting to know other students, besides those at Queen's. As time went on, we began to look for suitable parishes in which to begin our ministry after being ordained deacon. Canon Gribble, the principal, suggested to me that I might consider going to the diocese of Chelmsford, Essex. I think the Bishop of Chelmsford was appealing for more curates to serve in that huge diocese which took in a large part of East London, as well as the whole county of Essex. Without jumping ahead too much, I can just say here that the Vicar of Chigwell, near Epping Forest, the Revd Wilfrid Dickinson, was put in touch with me, at the Bishop's suggestion, with a view to my joining him as his curate. I had a very happy weekend with him and his family as a preliminary visit; but I had to be "a friend of the Vicar" as far as parishioners were concerned.

I attended a parish social evening, and had some difficulty in parrying questions that people were asking me about who I was. We had a guessing game that was a kind of variation of "What's my Line?" Everyone had an occupation pinned on their back, and they had to discover what it was by asking other people questions to which the only answers could be Yes or No. When I had worked out that the card on my back probably said "Professional Footballer", a parishioner came up and asked me who I was. Thinking her question was part of the game, I said "A professional footballer". That really caught her by surprise – she asked what team I played for (it's nice to think that I looked fit enough to make anyone think that that could possibly be my profession!). Then I had to do some humming and hawing, to try to get round the awkward risk of her guessing rightly why I had come to stay with the Vicar. Some people, I gather, did put two and two together!

Birmingham was of course, when I was there, and still is, a very important transport centre. Long-distance and local railway services are extremely comprehensive, based on the former LMS New Street station, and the former GWR Snow Hill station. In 1960 it took two hours to get from Birmingham to my home city of Bristol by train. That route then still had steam locomotives. The city of Birmingham I remember being very fully served by the smart dark blue and cream buses of Birmingham Corporation. There was some civic pride in that huge undertaking; and something of that pride spread to the citizens. Like most bus operators at that time Birmingham's transport was affected by difficulties of staff recruitment; I gathered that 120 buses were left idle every day, because there were insufficient drivers. That of course led to gaps in service; but where services were scheduled to be frequent, the omission of an occasional bus did not have serious effects – some people just had to wait a few minutes longer.

It was on the less frequent routes of many companies that the cutting out of time-tabled journeys caused much more hardship and anger. The corporation buses operated almost entirely within Birmingham city boundary. An exception was a group of two or three routes which were run jointly with West Bromwich Corporation buses, reaching places in that adjacent town. An unusual arrangement existed, whereby on buses of both operators it was necessary for through passengers to buy new tickets on reaching the Birmingham/West Bromwich boundary, so that both corporations got the revenue from travel within their own boundaries and not beyond.

For journeys between Birmingham and other places outside the city, Midland Red provided a wide range of services, some of them quite intensive. To protect Birmingham Corporation's revenue from fares, Midland Red did not carry passengers for journeys wholly within the city (or any who tried to use their buses for such journeys had a very hefty addition to the corporation's fare to pay!). The corporation buses' high frequencies meant that Midland Red's "protective" fares did not cause problems, as happened later in some other towns where a similar policy was followed – and passengers waiting for infrequent corporation buses were not at all pleased to see other companies' buses, which could have taken them to their destination, sailing past with empty seats. Birmingham Corporation had a fascinating "outer circle" route, following the ring road, and taking a long time to complete the circuit of the city; that useful route provided lots of inter-suburban journeys and connections.

Among the longer Midland Red routes from Birmingham were some with an X prefix to their route number – comparable perhaps to London's Green Line coaches, stopping less frequently than other buses. They went to Nottingham, Derby, Shrewsbury, Northampton, Leicester, Cheltenham, Gloucester, and maybe some other places. I sampled several of them. Midland Red was then all one company, with tentacles stretching from Hay-on-Wye to Grantham. It was some years later that it was to be pulled to pieces for doctrinaire reasons about which many were sceptical. However, I suppose the "rationalisations" did produce considerable economy of "duplicated" mileage; and it ended the "protective fares" arrangement.

One very memorable privilege that was mine in the brief period between my leaving Birmingham and being ordained deacon to serve as curate at Chigwell was to attend the Oberammergau Passion Play in August 1960. A party was got up by Queen's College to go there together; and much good fellowship was enjoyed. After the Passion Play we spent a few days at two Alpine places: Konigsee, with its impressive lake, near Berchtesgaden (from where we visited Hitler's hideout, the Eagle's Nest, accessible only by buses with special brakes and gears suitable for the extremely steep

Keep Me Travelling

approach); and a village near Innsbruck which we used as a base for some marvellous walks. We travelled by train on the overnight Tauern Express from Ostend to Munich; and returned from Innsbruck past Zurich's lake shimmering with reflected lights from the city, via Basle, where Switzerland, Germany and France all meet at the railway station, and through to Calais, I think, for the crossing to Folkestone, not Dover. On my return to Bristol, I had about ten days in which to get ready for the big change of life that was about to come.

CHAPTER 5

London Transport Buses and Tubes, Electric and Diesel BR Trains, two-wheels leg-powered and petrol-powered.

Before Ordination it is the custom to attend a retreat of a few days, which leads up to the Ordination service. Those ordained in Chelmsford diocese went to the lovely retreat house at Pleshey, in quiet Essex countryside. I have memories, and actually have kept notes, of a superb set of addresses there from Canon Sydney Evans, then Principal of Kings College, London. They really helped me sort out a lot of things in my mind on the eve of becoming a deacon and starting my first curacy at Chigwell. Of course I felt a bit nervous – but I can say with all honesty that right from the memorable Ordination Day, the Vicar of Chigwell could not have been more helpful and supportive to me. The Ordination was conducted by The Right Revd Falkner Allison, who was later to become Bishop of Winchester.

Each candidate had a private talk with him at the retreat house, and he was most encouraging, assuring me that I would be sure to be happy, with Wilfrid Dickinson as my vicar. When I had seen the Bishop a few months earlier, he had interviewed me in a taxi in London, on his way between two engagements – he was determined to make full use of his time! After the taxi ride we sat on a seat together by the Thames and he asked me to summarise briefly the Gospel according to Henry Ormerod! He had also asked me a lot about what I had gained from my time at Queen's College, Birmingham.

When I got to Chigwell, the vicar had clearly encouraged people to have me round to their homes. I got a lot of invitations, and received some very kind hospitality. That helped so much in getting to know the people of the parish in friendly and informal settings. You may wonder why Priscilla Mallinson has dropped completely out of the story since my first mention of her as my future wife when telling of Cambridge days. I was still in regular touch with her; but we went our own separate ways for several years. She took up teaching posts, including one in Cyprus at an RAF school. I will tell in due course of how we came back into close contact with each other, with the results that have already been told!

So many of the foundations of a curate's future ministry are laid in his (or her) first parish. At that particular time Wilfrid Dickinson's very traditional views about worship and Christian doctrine and discipline were, I think, right for me to absorb. When later I came to see some things in rather a different light, I had his firm convictions to measure any developments in my views by. The expectations that curates in their twenties are likely to spend quite a bit of their time in the company of the younger people of the parish certainly came true in my case. We did have some very capable and visionary people in the church congregations who were keen to develop ministry among young people, and I owe a very great deal to their insights that they shared with me when we were considering the lines along which any expansion of youth work might be planned. In fact we held a "youth weekend", led by a visiting priest who had outstanding expertise; and from that developed a full programme of ongoing activity. That incorporated an already existing midweek club night, and a Sunday evening programme was introduced, with much variety, designed to help teenagers to develop a more "mature" faith and Christian understanding.

I was also much engaged in the "Pathfinders" group that we established for those who felt a bit old for traditional "Sunday School". That again was possible only because of some excellent people in the parish who were prepared for the commitment that such a group required. A rather unusual kind of link with teenage boys was provided by the fact that the boarders at Chigwell School (a public school) attended the Sunday morning service at the parish church most weeks in term-time. To preach to any congregation is, of course, a big responsibility. To preach to a congregation made up partly of schoolboys who are in church by compulsion rather than choice makes that responsibility all the more daunting. The headmaster, who customarily read the lessons, was also sitting there. With memories of my Marlborough diary, I was very concerned to try to avoid my sermon, when it was my turn to preach, being dismissed as "dull" by the boys.

Wilfrid Dickinson had got the reputation with the school of always trying to get people to give more money to the church; and whenever that sort of appeal came up in any of his sermons, there was laughter from the boys! He did actually by example show me that a sermon in front of school pupils does not have to be a sort of stunt; sincerity and imagination go a long way in helping the Christian religion and the Bible to come alive for people of all ages. When the Dean of Pembroke College, Cambridge, whom I had known so well, came one Sunday to preach at Chigwell parish church, he said to me that it was extremely good for my future ministry to have the school boarders to address in church. He said, "When they're not there, pretend that they are!" A wise piece of advice, I think.

With the co-operation of the headmaster and chaplain of Chigwell School, a number of the boarders came to join in some of the church-based youth activities. That did at least give them the chance of meeting some girls! I know of one or two romances that began in Chigwell church life. We did actually have two churches; the modern daughter-church of St. Winifred served a residential area some way from the old village, where the parish church of St. Mary was situated. It also had a very good hall, which was the venue for Pathfinders and the Sunday night fellowship. When the vicar was on holiday, my Sunday programme could be as follows:

8.00 a.m.	Holy Communion. St. Mary's.
9.30 a.m.	Holy Communion, with hymns and address. St. Winifred's.

11.00 a.m.	Morning Prayer, sung, with sermon. St. Mary's.
12.15 p.m.	Shortened Holy Communion (for older people). St. Mary's.
2.45 p.m.	Pathfinders.
4.15 p.m.	Baptism, at either church.
5.30 p.m.	Evensong. St. Mary's.
6.45 p.m.	Evensong. St. Winifred's.
8.00 p.m.	Young People's Fellowship.

I was ready for bed after that! Usually, I had Mondays free; but if the vicar was away, funerals and other commitments could creep into them.

Chigwell, only twelve miles from central London, was served by London Transport trains and buses. Two stations, Chigwell and Grange Hill, were in the parish, both of them on the Woodford to Hainault branch of the Central Line of the Underground (though of course not underground out there). The Essex sections of the Central Line were largely based on former LNER lines from Liverpool Street, now taken over by London transport with tube trains that ran right through London to the west side at Ealing and Ruislip. The branch passing through Chigwell linked the two through routes. Except at peak hours passengers from Chigwell going into London, had to change at Woodford. A good service was provided. The number 10 London bus route came out to Chigwell; or rather a minority of buses on that route did, and they terminated in the real countryside a few miles further out at Abridge. That route was particularly useful for those

Keep Me Travelling

going to the good shopping centre at Leytonstone. AEC buses of the famous RT type (from Leyton garage) did most of the Abridge journeys; but variety was provided by a few journeys being covered by Leyland RTLs from Gillingham Street garage, near Victoria. Victoria Station was the southern terminus of route 10; in practice through running over the whole route took place only on a few early morning journeys, and on Saturday afternoons. On Sundays buses ran through from Abridge via Chigwell to London Bridge. At other times most of the number 10 buses that I saw in the parish were en route just between Abridge and Leytonstone. Another useful route was the 167, served by Loughton garage, running RTs between Debden, Loughton, Chigwell, and Ilford. I suppose Ilford was for Chigwell residents their main town if they were not going up to London; and Ilford station provided access to the Eastern Region lines to Southend, Chelmsford, and connections to places on the Norwich route.

I lived in rooms in two different houses in Chigwell during my time there. To go into London it was easiest from one of them to get the 10 bus to South Woodford Central Line Station, and from the other the 167 to Gants Hill station, as neither Chigwell nor Grange Hill stations were very near to where I was living. For local getting about I simply had a bicycle at this point in my career. It was in my next parish that I graduated to a motor-scooter, as I will explain.

After four years I moved on from Chigwell to my next post. When, at post-ordination training, etc. I heard the most awful stories about how some curates were treated by their vicars and parishioners, I felt that I had been extremely lucky to have gone to Chigwell to work with Wilfrid. I kept in touch with him; and when he died in 1998, his family invited me to lead prayers at a memorial service for him that was held at Chigwell parish church. He had left Chigwell a good many years before, but he had twenty-four years there, a good stint.

The parish consisted mainly of owner-occupied houses; and there were quite a number of very well-off people living there. However, there were also a number of council houses in parts of the parish, and some parishioners were far from being at all wealthy. I did have some concern that the two churches, which were quite well attended, hardly seemed to get the council house tenants, except for the occasional baptism, wedding or funeral. Later in my ministry, I did have very much higher proportions of relatively deprived people in the parishes I served; and discerning the most appropriate kind of ministry to them was extremely important.

After my first year at Chigwell as a deacon, I was ordained priest by Bishop Allison, Bishop of Chelmsford, in Chelmsford Cathedral, with a considerable number of other ordinands. Shortly afterwards, Bishop Allison took up his appointment at Winchester; and there came in his place to be Bishop of Chelmsford the Right Revd John Tiarks – the first Bishop to call me Henry! As a priest my ministry in Chigwell was extended, particularly in being authorised to celebrate Holy Communion. I also took my first wedding not long afterwards; and just before the bride came in, I suddenly noticed that our dear verger had put copies of the funeral service in all the pews instead of the wedding service! I was surprised that none of the guests who were already in their places in church had drawn my or the verger's attention to that!

I agreed with Wilfrid Dickinson that I would stay at Chigwell for a ten-day teaching mission that had been planned for September, 1964. It was led by Brother Reginald of the Society of St. Francis, with the help of two sisters of the Community of St. Margaret, East Grinstead, and two ordination candidates from Westcott House Theological College, Cambridge. I was very glad that I was still at Chigwell for that; it did somehow bring the parish together very well, and I learned quite a lot from the meetings that were held, where spiritual things were discussed in quite an informal setting, and people did feel able to talk about their faith and their difficulties regarding faith quite freely.

By the time of that mission, I had got fixed up with a second curacy, at Thundersley, a few miles from Southend-on-Sea, where I went in October, 1964. Bishop Tiarks thought that it would be a good parish, which would "amplify my experience", and so it turned out to be. It was not a "select" area in the way that much of Chigwell was. The people most actively involved in the life of the church were generally of a rather lower income bracket than at Chigwell; and informality was more the order of the day.

Everyone called me Henry from the start; I was teased a good deal – there was a lot of laughter and fun in church life, and social activities included such things as a men v. women cricket match, bowls on Southend sea front, men v. boys at football (the men having to wear wellingtons!), an annual parish concert (the ridiculous having more prominence than the sublime!), and quite a good programme for the young all through the year.

The Revd Leonard Woodcock was Rector, and again there were two places of worship with regular services. It was a very spread out area, not quite town and not quite country. A lot of new building was going on. The sweet little old parish church, belonging to the old village of Thundersley, was very considerably enlarged, and very tastefully too, during the time that I was there. All the interest and publicity surrounding that made the church a talking point in the community; and the opportunities provided by that major venture certainly did encourage more people to come to the church services.

It was a growing parish church-wise as well as population-wise. I had great respect for Leonard Woodcock, who was exceptionally gifted in many ways. He was a member of the Diocesan Children's Council; and his leading of worship when children were present was outstandingly good. I learned an enormous amount from him. I think he was ahead of his time in the way he brought children into the services in a light-hearted manner, but always with a clear teaching purpose.

He also applied to the Sunday School some new thinking about Christian instruction of children that was gaining ground at the time – "inductive" teaching, to use a technical term, relating the Bible and the Church to the children's experience and interests. That may have made considerable demands on Sunday School teachers, but I think the youngsters enjoyed it. I attended a national conference at Hereford on these developments in children's work, and subsequently tried, in cooperation with others involved, to put them into practice, both in Sunday School and club settings.

Thundersley, predominantly a residential area, was between the two parallel railway lines that linked London with Southend. From some parts of the parish the nearest station was Benfleet, on the Fenchurch Street line, now called C2C, and originally the London, Tilbury and Southend line. The northern part of Thundersley was nearer to Rayleigh station, on the old Great Eastern, from where trains went to Liverpool Street. A fair number of people from the area commuted to London each day. The rail services on both lines were frequent.

Southend Corporation ran its own bus service, with bright blue buses, and they came out to Thundersley on two different routes. Other buses passing through the parish were Eastern National, belonging to the large regional company which served much of Essex. In fact a co-ordination agreement had been reached between those two major bus operators, pooling receipts in proportion to the mileage that each ran within Southend and the adjacent local authority areas of Rochford, Rayleigh, Benfleet and Canvey Island. That was supposed to prevent "wasteful" competition, and also avoided "protective" fares on Eastern National routes. However, there were still the problems of recruiting and retaining staff for the buses. Eastern National seemed to have recurrent difficulties over industrial relations, with brief strikes from time to time, leaving Southend Corporation dreadfully overstretched on strike days. In November, 1967, with, as far as I remember, no warning to the public, we woke up one day to find no buses on the roads, of either Eastern National or Southend Corporation.

What had been simmering to bring that drastic action about nobody quite knew, except those directly involved. Southend Corporation tried to break the strike, by running some of its buses to an emergency timetable, driven by office staff, inspectors and other employees who were qualified to step in. Furthermore, they ran some of those buses with a crew of one on roads that did not normally have single-manning. It had involved some very quick modification of certain front-entrance, front-engined buses, so that the driver could, awkwardly, take fares. That caused some resentment among the crews who were on strike; and even more trouble erupted from them when Southend Corporation began to hire buses and coaches, with drivers, from other firms to increase the "emergency" services.

Some of these "pirate" buses, as they were accusingly called, were timed to run at what were normally Eastern National bus timings on the long Shoeburyness-Southend-Canvey route, a service that in normal times was jointly covered by the two operators. Anyhow the strike went on and on. The emergency time-tables left many roads uncovered, and frequencies were much reduced, with no evening or Sunday buses.

The public were angrily asking, "What's going on?" And there were many accusations of gross mismanagement. Though car ownership had grown a lot, there were very many people still dependent on the local bus services for getting about. When eventually the strike came to an end barely a week before Christmas, it transpired that a lot of bus staff had left and found other jobs; so the restored services were extremely unreliable. Eventually, I think, the two operators got together to introduce timetables that they could maintain with the human resources available. The public certainly preferred reliable services, even if scheduled to run less frequently, to services purporting to be more frequent, but with too many non-appearances of scheduled buses.

I mentioned earlier my personal transport being upgraded from pushbike to powered bike. I had been approached before leaving Chigwell over the idea that the parish might give me a scooter as a leaving present. I had never ridden any kind of motorcycle, and explained that while I greatly appreciated the generous thought, it might be better for me to see later whether it would be useful to have one. It didn't take me long to see that the distances I had to travel in Thundersley parish were a bit excessive for reliance on an ordinary bike. So after about two months I purchased, with money given me by Chigwell, a Vespa scooter.

It may seem funny to think now how lax the regulations then were over the use of powered two-wheelers. Helmets were not compulsory. You could pick up a motorbike from a dealer, and ride it away (with Lplates) even if you had never sat on one before. When I went to collect my scooter, the dealer did offer me a bit of tuition on private ground at his premises, which I was glad to accept. Scooters in those days did not have automatic transmission; so it was essential to practise getting the right coordination between the clutch, throttle and gears before venturing on to the road and joining the traffic.

I was a bit disconcerted when a young employee of the dealer, whom he had asked to get my bike out and check it over, had some difficulty in starting it (no electric starters on scooters then; you had to kick hard). I hoped I hadn't been "sold a pup!" Actually I quickly found that the machine started very easily, even on a cold morning, with the right knack. When I appeared in Thundersley parish on my Vespa, that caused some amusement to the younger element! The scooter gave me very good service for six and a half years, by which time it was pretty well worn out.

Priscilla Mallinson came back into the scene when I was at Thundersley. She completed her "tour of duty" in Cyprus, and had a teaching post at Felsted preparatory school, in Essex. Her parents' home was at Highgate, in north London; it was often most convenient for us to meet in London. We sometimes also saw each other in Chelmsford, situated between Felsted and Thundersley. We went on holiday together to Pennine country in August 1967 (where a friend of a friend, who knew me slightly, spotted us together!). Our engagement was announced on Hallowe'en; and we were married in

Highgate School Chapel on 3 February 1968. The reason for that venue for the wedding was that Priscilla's father was a long-established member of Highgate School's teaching staff. I had been living in lodgings in Thundersley (and in fact had lived in the house of an extremely nice and kind couple). The parish did not then have accommodation for a married curate. I had been there for over three years; so it seemed best to make a move.

The Bishop of Chelmsford asked if I would be willing to take a post on nearby Canvey Island. Though technically curate, I would have considerable responsibility, with charge of a daughter-church which served the eastern part of the island; and I would share with the vicar in the wider life of the church on the island, with particular input into the work with the younger generation. Priscilla and I were both very greatly struck by the friendly welcome we received from the vicar, the Revd John Fleetwood and his wife Joan, when we went to visit them, and they showed us round the island.

I say "island", because that is its name; you didn't have to get a ferry across from the mainland – there was a road bridge – but when you were on Canvey it somehow seemed to have quite a different feel about it. It was, and is, below sea level. The sea wall provided superb walks. The air was really good. We had no hesitation in accepting the post; and there was a small, but very adequate, house for us to occupy, near the church for which I was responsible, a mile and three-quarters from the Vicarage, and four miles from the bridge on to the mainland.

CHAPTER 6

Wedding car, Aircraft, Priscilla's Simca.

Not only had I never travelled in a wedding car before our wedding day, but I had never travelled in an aircraft either until our honeymoon. Priscilla and I had a week in Portugal, which felt really springlike in early February. We stayed at Monte Estoril, near the beautiful fishing port of Cascais, and only a short distance from Lisbon. Priscilla already knew something of my interest in transport; but I think she was a bit taken aback at my fascination with the railway and bus timetables in Portugal. A very efficient local railway provided regular services to Lisbon from where we were staying. We visited that fine city on more than one day, and memories came back to me of the time we had there as a port of call on our 1957 cruise.

Use of the trains and local bus services took us to other places of interest in the vicinity; and we hired a taxi for a tour of the impressive coastline. On the Sunday we attended the English church at Cascais (there were sufficient English people living around there to make the church viable); and the chaplain invited us to his house for drinks after the service. Our return to England saw our first night at Canvey Island, without any curtains in the house, so we had to undress in the dark! Priscilla and I quickly began to feel a sense of belonging to the Canvey community. There were very warm-hearted people there, quite unpretentious.

Of course it was an adjustment for us both; Priscilla did a bit of part-time teaching – I hope I did enough in the way of part-time domesticity! I have not yet mentioned Priscilla's talent as an artist, which had blossomed particularly during her time in Cyprus. Her friends said to me, "You must see that she is able to keep up her painting." In fact her artistic skills have been enormously useful to the parishes in which we have served over the years. Her designing of a cover for the Canvey parish magazine, called *The Bridge*, showing that old bridge over Benfleet Creek, Canvey's one link with the rest of England, was much appreciated – and it was a forerunner of many more magazine cover designs elsewhere.

Compared with Thundersley and Chigwell, Canvey seemed to contain rather an un-churched population. I suppose the majority of its inhabitants were not from any church background. Many had come there from east London. Houses were a bit cheaper than on the adjacent "mainland". There were large housing estates that accommodated people rehoused from Walthamstow and Dagenham Boroughs. There was some industry on Canvey, notably oil refineries and a natural gas terminal. Most people went to work off the island, either in the various industrial complexes elsewhere in south Essex, or in London. From Benfleet station, officially called, "Benfleet, for Canvey Island", the fastest electric trains reached Fenchurch Street in thirty-five minutes.

Mentioning transport, I might as well say a bit more about it at this point. The island, with its population then of some 20,000 people (double that now) was well served by buses of both Eastern National and Southend Corporation, being within their coordinated "Southend and District" area. The sporadic Eastern national one-day strikes still wouldn't go away; I put up a list at a major bus stop of the times when Southend Corporation buses could be expected on days when local Eastern National services were non-operative, and that seemed to be appreciated. Eastern National had a small depot on the island (now a transport museum), but its buses and crews spent most of their time off the island, on long routes shared with other depots to Southend and Shoeburyness, Basildon and Romford; and the majority of buses we saw on the island were from other depots sharing those same routes.

Before I left a reorganisation of services brought through buses on to Canvey from Wood Green in London every half-hour. One local route on the island served parts which the trunk services did not reach, and that was worked by Canvey depot. The only time when I used the Wood Green route as far as Gants Hill underground station, near Ilford. was not very satisfactory. There was a strike on British Rail; and I left very early in the morning without quite realising the congestion that we would meet on the roads as we got nearer London, as those who usually commuted by rail went by car instead. The double-deck bus I was in had some mechanical fault, and had to be taken out of service at Basildon. The only spare bus that Basildon depot could offer to continue the journey was a sixteen-year-old, five-cylinder-engined model, which really laboured with its increasingly full load of passengers on the occasional uphill stretches. Eventually, and with considerable relief, I changed to the Underground at Gants Hill, having arrived there much, much later than scheduled. It just went to show how dependent London and its satellite towns were on the railway systems operating normally.

I wasn't so dependent on public transport and my scooter at Canvey, because Priscilla had driven back with a friend across Europe to England on her return from her teaching post in Cyprus, in the little Simca car that she had bought in Cyprus. She still had it, and it provided useful mobility. Don't forget, we had to go four miles to reach the bridge that led off the island. Southend pier was clearly visible from the Point, at the eastern end of Canvey, near where we lived; but by road it was thirteen miles to get to Southend; the first four miles of the journey were in the opposite direction, on the island. Actually, to get into Southend by public transport it was certainly quicker to get off the bus at Benfleet station and change to one of the frequent trains, which took thirteen minutes to Southend from there. To stay on the bus all the way took much longer, and some buses went by a roundabout route.

To get back to more spiritual matters, it was soon evident to me that considerably more people on Canvey went to church than I originally thought, when I realised that only a fairly small proportion of them went to the

Church of England. There were churches of most denominations on the island, and an extremely good spirit of co-operation between them. For the first time in my ministry I found myself working in close fellowship with the Free Churches and the Roman Catholics. All the ministers and priests were good friends; and we had united services, Bible studies, social gatherings, etc. – also a very good concerted effort for the Christian Aid Week house-to-house collection. (At neither Chigwell nor Thundersley were ecumenical relationships so developed, nor was there the wide range of churches that I found on Canvey.)

The fact that Canvey Island had its own very clearcut identity, I think, gave the clergy a rather more clearly recognised public position in the community. The island had its own local newspaper, and the churches figured prominently in that. The extremely likeable and capable Methodist minister, the Revd John Ducker, who often came to Church of England weekday services, I met again some years later, when he was appointed to a senior Methodist post near our parish in Swindon in the 1980s. The Roman Catholic priest, Father Godfrey, was great fun; I had never previously known a Roman Catholic priest anything like so well.

The enormous growth of housing on Canvey Island had rather left the little old parish church of St. Catherine in the wrong place; and it was nothing like big enough for the actual, let alone the potential, congregation. A new parish church, dedicated to St. Nicholas, had been built in 1960, eight years before we came. It was of a most striking design, of Dutch influence, appropriate because the island had been originally drained and made habitable by the Dutch. There was a sweet little Dutch museum, which told the story of the island.

Incidentally, Priscilla and I attended the fortieth anniversary service of the consecration of St. Nicholas church in the year 2000. St. Anne's Church, in Leigh Beck, the eastern part of the island where we lived, had been built early in the twentieth century to serve what was then a rural area, separate from the main centre of population on the island. In fact, shortly after we left, St. Anne's was demolished and completely rebuilt, to be more suitable and larger for the rapidly developing housing area that it served.

In the days when we were there, there was still a considerable demand for the baptism of infants; and baptisms were held every Sunday. We tried to maintain pastoral links with the families, and to prepare them as well as we could for the service and the ongoing responsibilities of bringing up the children as Christians. John Fleetwood's policy was to "build bridges of friendship", and for that he became well known and respected. There were also a lot of weddings. Again we regarded suitable preparation of the couples as important, and did the best we could for them, keeping in touch with those who continued to live on the island, and trying to notify the vicars of other parishes where they were going to reside. Funerals, when you have a large population in a parish, were, and still are, likely to be time-consuming. It's not just the funeral service, but the pastoral relationship with the family, that counts for such a lot. We got very friendly with the first-class funeral directors who served the area.

From a family point of view, our time on Canvey was very important and happy for Priscilla and me. Our daughter Sarah and our elder son Michael were both born when we were there, and were aged three and twenty-months when we left in June 1972. Having young children made a big difference to our relationships with many people in the community. We received much kindness and friendly interest in the children's progress. It was important that I should try to get parish and family responsibilities in proper balance, and tried to reorder my work patterns a bit to be available to Priscilla and our children sufficiently regularly. Sarah was baptised at St. Anne's, and Michael at St. Nicholas', both by John Fleetwood – Michael was one of seven baptised at the same service.

Priscilla's and my memories of Canvey Island from this distance in time are a jumble of people, places and events. Some seem to stand out particularly strongly. Among those is Miss Gwen Evans, organist at St. Anne's, a clergyman's daughter, who had lived on Canvey for years in the same house, which must have been quite isolated when she first lived there. She had run a small private school; and those I knew who had been pupils there had quite a pride in that fact. She had the sweetest imaginable disposition, and was most welcoming to Priscilla and me. Another tower of strength at St. Anne's was Miss Ethel Allbutt. She ran the Guide company attached to St. Anne's Church, and also, in conjunction with Miss Evans, the Sunday School. She took enormous responsibility as sacristan-cum-verger for St. Anne's. It would have been unthinkable for any service to be held there without her being present.

My coming, and my idiosyncrasies, may not have been entirely easy for her to adjust to. However, we did build up a good working relationship that developed into quite close friendship. Ethel was very keen that the sick should be regularly prayed for by name, and I inherited a prayer meeting (twice a month, I think), at which this was done – and the prayer was supplemented by decisions about visiting and caring for those prayed for. I do remember at my first Sunday service at St. Anne's finding the Holy Communion wine flask didn't pour very easily; and when Ethel noticed that a little bit of wine had got on to the altar cloth, her immediate remark to me was, "I'll kill you dead!" Fortunately, she didn't; but I daresay you can imagine my feeling a bit uncomfortable when subsequently I had to handle that awkward flask!

Mention of the Guides brings me to memories of extremely well led Baden Powell uniformed groups on Canvey, based at both St. Nicholas' and St. Anne's. The Scouts' District Commissioner was Mr Arthur Bishop, a Justice of the Peace, churchwarden of St. Nicholas', and a man outstandingly active in the community. His daughter Josie was married to Mr Tony Peck, who was scoutmaster of the St. Nicholas' troop; and the whole family were very fully involved in scouting at district level, probably higher as well. Tony and Josie were several decades later to receive well-deserved honours from the Queen for their services to scouting. In charge of the St. Anne's Scouts was Mr Berry, churchwarden of St. Anne's, supported by very capable assistant leaders. The troop had an active and keen parents' association, who arranged all sorts of social and money-raising events. They always invited Priscilla and me to them; and they enabled us to get to know a wider circle of people informally. I think our appearance as tramps at a tramps' supper succeeded in breaking any ice that was left to be broken!

At both churches the Guides were supplemented by companies of the Girls' Brigade – so great was the demand for that sort of activity. At St. Anne's we tried to make the monthly parade service for the uniformed groups into a service rather more on the lines of what I had picked up from Leonard Woodcock at Thundersley. Priscilla, with her artistic skills, produced some very helpful visual aids. While of course wanting to retain the dignity proper to any church service, we tried to find the right blend with informality – and after a time we had people coming to the parade services who had no connection with the uniformed groups or Sunday School.

The Revd John Fleetwood had to wait to go to a London hospital for a hip operation. Not knowing quite how long he might have to wait, I said that I would not leave the parish until he had had his operation, and was back in full harness. I could see that the size and position of Canvey Island, with its limited access, could make things very difficult if there were no Church of England clergyman there for some length of time; and I think the Bishop was greatly relieved by my offer to stay. Bishop John Tiarks retired in 1971, and was succeeded by Bishop John Trillo. When he came to speak to the Southend deanery clergy chapter, to which we belonged, he spoke with me for quite a long time, asking a good deal about Canvey and looking forward to paying a visit when the Vicar was able to get back to work again. He, and the Bishop of Bradwell, the Right Revd Neville Welch, who had a special responsibility for the south-eastern side of Essex, both said that they would try to find a suitable parish for me to go to as vicar – but that it might also be a good thing for me to keep an eye on vacancies in other dioceses advertised in the *Church Times*. That was becoming a more and more common practice.

I spotted (actually I think John Fleetwood noticed it first, and rang me up to draw it to my attention) an advertisement placed by Emmanuel College, Cambridge, who were looking for a vicar for the parish of Stanground, on the outskirts of Peterborough, of which the college was the patron. Anomalously it was in the diocese of Ely, not Peterborough. The literature that I received from Emmanuel College in response to my enquiry made Priscilla and me feel that this might well be a suitable place to which to go. There was the nucleus of the old village, with the beautiful medieval parish church of St. John the Baptist; but the village had expanded greatly into being in effect a suburb of Peterborough. New housing was being built; and a new church had been built and opened only the year before to serve a developing area further out from Peterborough, straddling the Whittlesey road. A detailed form of application that I had to send in to Emmanuel College, with the names of referees, resulted in my being called for interview at Emmanuel College in March 1972. Things moved very quickly from there; the college offered me the "living", subject to the agreement of the Bishop of Ely and of the churchwardens of the parish.

On my first visit to Stanground I went on my own (it would have been difficult for Priscilla, with the children); and I walked from Peterborough railway station the two and a half miles to the churchwarden's house. He and other church officers who had gathered there were quite astonished at my walking from the station – I think it counted in my favour, though I did it to get the feel of the place and its surroundings better. I picked up on that visit a sense that relationships between the old and the new church were not entirely harmonious.

That problem had been a bit exacerbated by the moving of the vicarage from a large house near St. John's church to a semi-detached modern house close to St. Michael's, the new church. It was thought to be much closer to the main centre of population of the parish. I could see that there were some extremely loyal and committed people who had the churches' work very close to their heart, and who were seeking fresh ways of reaching out to the growing population.

A retired priest who lived in Peterborough was taking main responsibility for the maintenance of the worshipping life of the churches during the vacancy, and was taking weddings, baptisms and funerals, with associated pastoral care. I got the sense that people would be sorry to lose him when a new vicar came; and I realised that some working agreement with him would be sensible and fair.

Anyhow, the message that the Stanground church officers would be willing to have me as their vicar reached me from the Bishop of Ely; and he then asked me to go to Ely to see him. He was the Right Revd Edward Roberts, and a more charming reception than I got from him at his house would be difficult to imagine. We did have some connections already, in that he had also been educated at Marlborough College, where he had known, quite well as a fellow-pupil, my father-in-law; and my uncle (at whose prep school I had spent that term before national service, as described earlier) had actually shared a study with him. It was then early April, and Bishop Roberts said that he wanted the vacancy at Stanground filled as soon as possible. He suggested there and then the date of 8 June for my institution and induction. I hadn't expected to go quite so soon. Bishop Roberts wrote to John Fleetwood to ask if he would accept only two months' notice of my leaving, rather than the statutory three months.

Priscilla and I had to get our skates on in order to be ready to move by the appointed date. Our cat had kittens a fortnight before our moving day. That added some complications! They all moved into Stanground vicarage with us – and we managed to get homes for them in the

Peterborough area, except for one which Tony and Josie Peck (already mentioned) came to our new parish to collect. I think we left a bit of ourselves behind on Canvey Island, after four and a quarter years there. It had been an unforgettable experience ministering in that "unusual" community – and I moved on with the benefit of many lessons that I had learned there.

CHAPTER 7

Austins, Hondas, InterCity 125s, the "National Bus Company".

Moving to a parish where I would be "incumbent" and would be expected to offer a higher degree of leadership than had so far been required of me, was in some ways quite a daunting experience; however, the very friendly welcome that we received at Stanground made our adjustment to our new situation smoother than I had dared to hope we would find it. I had not forgotten some words which I heard from a visiting speaker at theological college, to this effect: "People generally give a new vicar about four months before they decide whether or not to stay with him. During those four months he will be expected to get to know the regular church people sufficiently well to be able to pray for them meaningfully – and to know anything of particular importance about individuals and families associated with the church. The people will hope that he will know how to make them laugh. A fairly light touch, on the whole, is appreciated. The kind of friendliness that goes a long way is not gushing or unctuous – but an obvious sincerity of the pleasure of being with people."

Of course a new vicar doesn't know at first hand the general ethos that his predecessor's ministry generated; but one picks up a good deal from conversations, and from observation of people's approach to worship and their expectations of preaching. It is important to be sensitive to people's personal spiritual disciplines, and, whatever one's own churchmanship may be, to conduct worship in such a way that those with a high-church tradition in the congregation are not offended by seeming irreverence, and that those with a more low-church tradition do not feel deprived of the kind of Bible teaching to which they look to build them up in the Christian faith and life. The ministry of word and sacrament need to be kept in the right balance, I'm sure.

I'm not saying that I succeeded in getting everything right along those lines. I learned from my mistakes and insensitivities. I annoyed a few people, quite unintentionally, by appearing to do some things rather differently from my conscientious and capable predecessor, and from the highly respected retired priest who had done so much to keep the parish life and worship going so well during the interval before I arrived. The old parish church and the new daughter-church had very different atmospheres about them. Some people attended not the church nearer to where they lived, but the one in which they were able to feel more at home.

I found in the parish that there was considerable demand for Baptisms and Weddings; and a fair number of funerals were held too. All these involved considerable pastoral responsibility. Also, young people were requesting Confirmation in quite large numbers, and that continued throughout my time at Stanground. It seemed so important to find ways of giving them the teaching which was necessary for that big step in the Christian life, and at the same time make them feel at ease and in a happy frame of mind. I latterly gave the Confirmation candidates a choice each week of a weekday after school or a Saturday morning for preparation (I didn't like to call it "classes"). It may look as if it gave me more work – but in fact it largely avoided "absenteeism" on account of other commitments that young people had. We also had adult Confirmation candidates, whose preparation was of course held separately from the youngsters.

The whole question of integrating the younger generation in the life of the church and training them for Christian responsibility in life occupied much of my concern. At St. Michael's, the daughter-church, we started a system (which I think is now quite commonplace) by which children could come in for the beginning part of the Holy Communion service, go into the adjacent hall for the middle part to receive teaching and engage in activity appropriate to their age, and then rejoin the congregation for the last part of the service, coming up to the altar for a blessing at the time of Communion. About three times a year we had a "Children's Eucharist", with a presentation by the boys and girls of what they had been doing in their Sunday groups during the previous month or two. That went down very well; it brought the children's work to the attention of other people, and helped the children to feel part of the "all-age" church family.

Ventures of that sort could only be attempted thanks to the extremely loyal and capable support of a group of adults and older teenagers, who were prepared to make the necessary commitment of their time and efforts. The parish church of St. John had a Sunday School that met separately from the adult congregation. We tried to find ways in which they could meet on occasions, and discover a bit about each other. The uniformed Baden-Powell groups paraded at Holy Communion at the parish church most months – and later another group of Guides and Brownies came to the daughter-church. Again, I felt it important, but did not always find it easy, to accommodate them side by side with the adult congregation, and make them feel comfortable and interested. A few adult communicants were not quite ready at that time for the adaptations of parts of the set service that I really felt were desirable in the circumstances – so much of the impact of the act of worship depended on finding a right balance between dignity and informality. Priscilla's art work proved most useful time and again.

While I was at Stanground the new experimental forms of worship were coming in; and the *Alternative Service Book*, of 1980, was published in my last year there. The church council had some quite heated discussions about whether we should use the new "Series 3" Holy Communion; it was a quite radical departure from Series 1 and 2, in that it used modern language, and addressed God as "You", not "Thou." The decision that we would change to the modern service upset some people – and provision was made for the more conservative Series 2 to be used at the 8 a.m. service on Sundays (which alternated between the two churches), and for the Prayer Book to be reintroduced for a midweek Holy Communion each Wednesday. We also kept to the Prayer Book for Sunday Evensong; but on the fifth Sunday of the month (about four times a year) we had a "Guest Service" in the evening, which varied in form, usually as some kind of variation on Songs of Praise, with a particular theme, and with Biblical and non-Biblical readings.

One that stands out in my memory, which went down particularly well, was on the theme of "The Church's Care from the Cradle to the Grave", with bits of the service and hymns devoted to baptism, confirmation, marriage, ministry to the sick and infirm, and bereavement and funerals. Occasionally, we devised a service from hymns chosen by the people from the congregation, who could introduce them if they wished. We were lucky with our loyal organists at both churches; Mr Dennis Pratt, at St. John's, was also choirmaster of the four-part choir which we had; he also took the St. Michael's choir practices – there we had for some years a choir made up entirely of young people. I don't think auditions for joining it were very thorough – but it didn't matter if the good singers "carried" one or two primary school children who could only sing bass, or who most certainly would not have been selected for their school's choir! Mrs Janet Robinson took the post of organist there, and was very loyal and competent.

Mentioning the schools, we had a Voluntary Controlled Church of England Primary School in the old Stanground village area. I had a good deal to do with it, as chairman of the governors for much of my time there; and each Friday morning I went to lead a short service (I didn't awfully like the word "assembly"), benefiting often from visual aids that Priscilla had prepared. For a week or so one year the school caretakers in the locality were called out on strike over some issue. The headmaster of St. John's School refused to close the school (unlike many head teachers who felt that they had no option but to keep their school closed). My job (which nobody on the school staff was allowed to do) was to open the school each morning and lock it each afternoon. The school caretaker (who I don't think approved of the strike) was quite willing for me to do that. It was in the summer term, when no heating was required. If other school caretakers got to know, I wondered whether I ought to go equipped for self-defence!

Before returning to various aspects of work and family life at Stanground, I will include a bit now on the transport situation. I always felt that Peterborough was something of a boundary town, where south-east England (the London commuter belt), East Anglia and the East Midlands all met, with their very different characteristics. Stanground was within the catchment area of the important InterCity railway station of Peterborough. Express trains between London (Kings Cross) and Edinburgh passed through Peterborough, though not many of them stopped there. However, quite a number of other expresses between Kings Cross and places in north-east England did call at Peterborough; and so there was a frequent and fast service to London.

Keep Me Travelling

Points north were also easily accessible. East-west trains included a regular Norwich to Birmingham semi-fast service; and to get to Bristol from Peterborough the recommended and cheapest route was via Birmingham, not London. Local trains served Cambridge, Spalding, Stamford, and intermediate stations on the London route. The main-line services from Kings Cross were gradually upgraded to the new InterCity 125 type high-speed diesel trains during the latter part of my time. On some timings Peterborough could then be reached in forty-seven minutes from London. Peterborough commuters took less time to get to work in London than did some who travelled in from outer London suburbs.

As far as buses were concerned, I renewed my acquaintance with the Eastern Counties Omnibus Company, which I had got to know well at Cambridge in the 1950s. By now Eastern Counties, like most of the major regional bus operators in England and Wales, had become part of the National Bus Company. Standardised liveries were coming in when I moved to Stanground in 1972. All "NBC" buses were painted in either a shade of "poppy-red" or "leaf-green".That meant that companies lost much of their distinctive identities for the sake of a dubious "sameness". In fact in Peterborough the red Eastern Counties buses dominated the scene; but there were also green United Counties NBC buses running into the city on routes from Northamptonshire towns. Non-NBC buses included those of Delaine, in their mainly blue colours, coming in from Bourne; and two small operators, Morleys and Canhams, ran between

Peterborough and Whittlesey, in the Fen country, dovetailed with the Eastern Counties services on the same route, to provide a combined service every twenty minutes. That route served the part of Stanground where we lived. Morleys' buses generally went on beyond Whittlesey marketplace to provide a town service serving most parts of Whittlesey. Some Eastern Counties journeys continued through to March. Other bits of the extensive built-up area of Stanground were served by Peterborough city services run by Eastern Counties, and one route went on to Farcet and Yaxley every half-hour. Several times a day buses ran through Stanground en route between Peterborough and Ramsey, extended to Huntingdon on Saturdays jointly with United Counties.

So we were pretty well served; and most certainly there were many non-car-owners in Stanground, for whom the regular bus services were a lifeline. Eastern Counties still standardised on the very reliable (if in some cases a bit underpowered) Bristol-type buses. The new double-deckers that came in, in large numbers, during the 1970s were of the Bristol VR (rear-engined) type, which I liked very much. They were much more powerful than the older buses they replaced. Also Peterborough began to receive some of the newly developed Leyland National large-capacity single-deckers. Their thirst for fuel caused a bit of a shock, I think, to the depot managers at first; and many in the bus industry regretted that their coming on the market caused the cessation of production of the very popular, smooth, reliable and comparatively economical Bristol RE

53-seater single-deckers. By the 1970s REs had largely replaced double-deckers on longer inter-town routes in many parts of the country. As the 1970s progressed, so conductors became more and more a vanishing species. All single-deckers, and front-entrance, rear-engined double-deckers, lent themselves well to driver-only operation, with people paying their fare as they boarded.

Our own main transport took the form of an Austin mini-traveller soon after we got to Stanground; Priscilla sold her Simca. I had already replaced my 1964 Vespa with a 1971 Honda bike, with semi-automatic transmission (gearchange, but no clutch); I kept that until 1979. It was very useful for Priscilla and me to be able to be independent of each other as far as personal transport was concerned – and for short journeys around the parish and city the Honda was more cost-effective (particularly in view of the fact that parishes were by then instructed by church authorities to refund their clergy their travel costs incurred in their work).

When eventually the Honda that had given such good service needed replacing, I became unstuck through purchasing an almost new machine, of a make which I had better not mention. It was offered at a very attractive price; and I quickly saw why its previous owner had got rid of it so quickly! The mixing of oil with the petrol for its 2-stroke engine had to be done terribly accurately, or there would be real trouble – a tiny bit too much oil, and the exhaust would smoke, and the sparking plug be liable to getting oiled up; a tiny bit too little oil, and there would develop an alarming smell of overheating, with the risk of the engine seizing. The magneto for generating electricity was so weak that the engine would not tick over with the lights switched on. After dark I had to be very careful to rev the engine sufficiently at traffic lights or other hold-ups to prevent it from stalling. While it started quite readily when warm, or, with the choke, when cold, it was not at all easy to start when lukewarm – I often hoped I had not left it standing too long. If you look up in the Bible, Revelation, chapter 3, verse 15, you will find the words addressed to the church at Laodicea, "I wish that you were either cold or hot". Laodicea might have been a suitable name for my bike! Anyhow, after seven months I was thankful to have another Honda instead – what a contrast to the cheaper end of the market!

To move to issues of more spiritual significance, the co-operation with other churches that had been such a valuable feature of the church life at Canvey continued and developed when I was at Stanground. I got to know a number of clergy and people of various churches in the Peterborough area, particularly through the Peterborough and District Council of Churches. I was appointed Hon. Secretary of the Unity Sub-committee of that body; and we were engaged in organising a number of processions of witness, special united services, etc. We produced an ecumenical cycle of prayer for all the churches and Christian organisations in and around Peterborough, which was widely used. Getting to know the Roman Catholic priests of the city, I found that some difficulties were caused, particularly to people without their own transport, by there being no Roman Catholic place of worship on the side of Peterborough where we lived. After discussions and correspondence with diocesan officials, the Roman Catholic authorities, and our own church council, agreement was reached that there should be Roman Catholic mass each Sunday in our daughter-church of St. Michael at a time when the building would not otherwise be used. That brought tremendous benefits all round.

Members of the Roman Catholic congregation helped with the cleaning of the church and provision of flowers. They gave support too to money-raising efforts. A sum agreed by both parties was paid to the church council by the Roman Catholics on a regular basis for their use of the building, heating, etc. (The Anglican parish of course remained responsible for the maintenance of the church building, and paying of bills.) Also, on certain occasions in the year, we would hold a joint service with the Roman Catholics, on a weekday, such as the Patronal Festival of St. Michael and All Angels. During my time two different Roman Catholic priests had pastoral responsibility for their congregation; and I was able to establish very good relationships with them both. When we left, the Roman Catholic congregation at St. Michael's gave me a present, which was very much appreciated.

Another development of considerable importance followed from the retirement of the vicar of the neighbouring parish of Farcet in 1976. The diocese of Ely did not think Farcet was big enough to justify having its own full-time vicar again. Stanground was expanding. I knew the Farcet people were wondering when the diocese would make up its mind what to do; and after some conversation with Farcet church officers, who approved this idea, I wrote to the Bishop of Ely to suggest that Farcet might be brought into a closer relationship with Stanground, and that maybe a priest-in-charge of Farcet church could be appointed, who would also share a bit in the work in Stanground. The Bishop wrote back with much enthusiasm, and said that he would put further investigation into the idea in the hands of the Archdeacon of Huntingdon (the Ven. David Young, soon to be Bishop of Ripon).

Anyhow, with a lot of legal entanglements and disentanglements, a scheme was prepared, by which Stanground and Farcet, while still remaining separate parishes, would be served by a Team Ministry – to begin with, just two clergy, but more could be added if thought desirable. I would be appointed Team Rector (so our house would become the Rectory, rather than the Vicarage – though when someone suggested it should be "The Victory", someone else thought "The Wreckage" would be a more suitable name!). The Archdeacon suggested that I should put an advertisement in the *Church Times* to try to find a suitable Team Vicar, who would live in Farcet Vicarage, be chairman of Farcet church council, take main responsibility there, but also be part of the ministerial team over the whole area of both parishes. Replies to the advertisement opened my eyes to the fact that there were considerable numbers of "unemployed" Church of England clergy around the country. I felt sorry for some who wrote most pathetic letters, desperate for a job. The Archdeacon and I together made a short list. I was concerned that the size and state of Farcet Vicarage might put off some prospective clergy and their wives. Parishioners did a good job in trying to make it look reasonably presentable.

I was very glad when we were able to appoint the Revd David Boxall to the post of Team Vicar. He and his wife Jen were very sporting in being willing to take on the living quarters that were to be theirs – and in fact they looked at its possibilities imaginatively. David had incidentally been curate of Thundersley, Essex, several years after I had left there – and a number of Thundersley people, including the Rector, the Revd Leonard Woodcock, whom I had served, came to his Licensing. David's coming proved to be thoroughly beneficial to both parishes. He took on some very imaginative work with young people, making use of part of the large Farcet Vicarage – and some from Stanground, as well as Farcet, became involved. With some help and guidance from him some people of Stanground parish established a well-run club for 11-plus boys and girls in St. Michael's hall (which had been used as a temporary church before the fine new church was opened in 1971).

Nobody can be everybody's cup of tea – I certainly am not! – and David's modernity of outlook was found by some to take a bit of getting used to. I think the key must always be mutual respect, and recognition that different people (including different clergy) have different things to offer. I also had some help from the Revd William

Wheeler, whose ministry in Stanground in the months before I came had been so much valued. As a retired priest, he had links with a number of churches; but he continued to minister a certain amount in ours – and he baptised our third child, of whose arrival the next paragraph will tell. I had to have another "Institution", to be made Team Rector; and the Bishop of Ely (by then the Right Revd Peter Walker, whom I found just as friendly as Bishop Edward Roberts) braved the February snow of 1978 to come over and perform that "legal nicety" at the evening service at St. John's one Sunday.

Our daughter Sarah and our son Michael reached school age at Stanground. Both of them went to Oakdale County Primary School, which served the part of the parish where we lived (the church school of St. John's was some distance away). Oakdale always seemed to be a very well controlled school, and it laid good foundations for both children. It contained both infant and junior departments. I did think that being at a local school enabled our children to get to know the children who lived around us better than if they went to school elsewhere. When Sarah joined the choir of St. Michael's church, some of her school friends joined too! She and Michael, inevitably, I suppose, got a bit of stick for being a clergyman's children. However, they coped with that extremely well – and they found plenty of congenial boys and girls there. We got to know some families well through our children.

On 19 February 1979, Peter Ormerod emerged into this world. The blizzard conditions at the time when

Priscilla had to go into hospital led the midwife to advise me to read up a bit about midwifery! Fortunately, however, an ambulance got through; and I was tremendously relieved when she was there. As at Canvey Island, so at Stanground, we found that having a baby brought us closer to a lot of people. Much interest was shown, much help was offered; and the two older children (by now aged nine and eight) were given a good deal of hospitality by kind people in the parish. While my responsibilities as Rector rather precluded me from having "paternity leave", yet for a time I tried to be as available as possible at home, and some aspects of church work I put aside for a while. David and William stepped in to cover some of my duties.

The time came when I had to think, "How long ought I to remain at Stanground?" Priscilla and I also had to consider where we could most suitably go next. As it was, we stayed at Stanground for a little over nine years, until August 1981. A major consideration relating to our next move was the fact that my mother, who was by then widowed, was living on her own at Bristol, in the same house where I had grown up, and her health was not all that good. My brother William lived at Poole, Dorset, a good deal nearer to her than we were; he was a doctor in general practice there, following in our father's steps. I wrote to the Bishop of Bristol to inquire whether there was any parish in his diocese where it might be suitable for us to go. He put me in touch with the Lord Chancellor's ecclesiastical office, with a view to their considering me for a vacant parish of which the Lord

Chancellor was patron. It was not in Bristol, but in Swindon, in the eastern extremity of Bristol diocese. We realised that if we did go there we would be much nearer to my mother, about an hour away by road via the M4.

Literature that we were sent showed that this Swindon parish consisted almost entirely of post-war housing estates, built largely to accommodate Londoners, at a time when Swindon was deliberately being made into an "expanding town" and its industrial base being greatly widened. It had traditionally been largely a "one industry" town, namely the Great Western Railway works. Though many residents had by 1981 bought their houses, the parish was all originally council housing. The kinds of social problems that are common in large estates of that type the literature told us existed in these estates of "Parks and Walcot". Was I the right sort of person to go there as Rector? Was it fair to our children to be set in that environment? Those questions of course occupied our minds.

Anyhow, an invitation reached me to go to 10 Downing Street, where the Lord Chancellor's ecclesiastical office was situated. That was an experience in itself. I had to show my letter to the policeman at the door; and I was given a tour of the building, including the Cabinet Room, though I didn't catch sight of the sitting tenant, Margaret Thatcher! The genial appointments secretary who served the Lord Chancellor gave me a very unchallenging interview, and never really got down to the matter of how I would hope to approach the work if I were appointed. I think I'm not being unfair if I say that the Bishop of Malmesbury (suffragan of Bristol) who subsequently interviewed me kept our meeting on a pretty superficial level as well. I got the impression that the Lord Chancellor and the diocese were anxious to get the vacancy filled.

Meeting key church people for the first time in the parish certainly showed me that there was a devoted and hard-working core, and that the "plant" was quite good. The next thing was an "official" interview within the parish, chaired by the Archdeacon of Swindon, which Priscilla was required to attend as well. I'm still doubtful whether it is really quite right to take the wife into account when an appointment of a clergyman is made to a parish (I don't know whether female vicars' husbands are vetted in a similar way!). Anyhow, it meant that we both met people with whom we would be working. The ministerial team included an absolutely first-class team vicar, the Revd Stephen Bessent, who had primary responsibility for Walcot and St. Andrew's church there; also a very conscientious woman worker, who was a licensed reader. The local Methodist minister attended the interview, because this was a Local Ecumenical Project; and the churches had pledged themselves to work together. The LEP also included the Roman Catholic Church of the Holy Family, situated on the boundary of the parish, and serving a much wider area of east Swindon.

As I will explain, following on from my experiences at Stanground, the ecumenical dimension proved to be very important and productive at Swindon. Soon after

Henry (right) aged 15 with his parents and brother William, in the south of France, April 1950.

Henry with Sarah and Michael, Canvey Island, 1971.

Keep Me Travelling

A musical background to lunch at Chamonix, August 1987.

Legoland, Billund, Denmark (before there was one in England).
August 1989. Peter in car 23.

Upstairs in the Tel Aviv – Jerusalem Egged Bus. April 1993.

A remarkable car registration. Bardolino, northern Italy, August 1993.

The Victorian Weekend, North Wingfield. June 1993.

Exploring Norwegian Fjords. August 1994.

With Tess, a dog dumped at the Rectory at Swindon. and a lovely companion for 14 years – at her longest-stay home, North Wingfield. (Photo by Mr Lawrence Marshall, Sarah's father-in-law).

Sarah and Norman leaving St. Lawrence's Church, North Wlngfield, after their marriage service. August 1997.

The diminutive, and absolutely lovely, church at Alkerton, in the Ironstone Benefice, near Banbury.

The Horley newspaper delivery round had to be done in all weathers. (Photo by Mr. Tim Allitt, of Horley).

At Horley Vicarage. Sarah and Norman with their first child, Joseph, and Priscilla with her first grandchild.

Henry and Priscilla at some location in the Lake District, April 2004.

Highgate, London. Priscilla (with a hairstyle many liked a lot) and her father, Theodore Mallinson, well into his 90s.

Theodore at his 95th birthday party in London.

The area around Grasmere wasn't very warm in April 2004 but Priscilla and Peter were enjoying a walk through the lovely scenery.

On a circuit of Chester city walls. A bracing autumn day in 2004.

that joint interview I received an official invitation from the Lord Chancellor's office to accept appointment as Team Rector, and a similar letter from the Bishop of Bristol. Priscilla and I decided that this seemed right – but I still had a lot to learn, and some of that learning was not to be without some pain.

CHAPTER 8

Motorways, Several Aircraft, Cross Channel Ferries.

After a very nice send-off from Stanground, we arrived at Swindon. A serious hiccup, however, was vandalism in the house where we were to live. It was just a little bit set back from the road; and shortly before we moved in, the sight that met the eyes of a churchwarden who was checking things over was horrific. In the cupboard under the stairs was a lot of burnt paper. Luckily any fire did not penetrate beyond that cupboard. Wallpaper that been newly put up was cut and scribbled on. Some decorator's materials left in the house were splattered around. The telephone was cut. We could, however, get in on the due day, and some hasty repairs and redecoration were put in hand just before our arrival. We were made to feel very anxious about the future, and particularly concerned for our children's welfare and safety. When the removal van arrived with our stuff, a whole lot of boys clustered round; and some of them actually helped to carry furniture and effects into the house. I thought that was a bit of cheek.

It was still the school summer holidays, and children were left hanging around without much to do. It was soon clear that the particular close in which the vicarage was situated, very near to the Church of St. John the Baptist (built in 1960), was a haunt where a gang regularly gathered; and it was just by the main shopping precinct that served the estate. Naturally our children were wary about running the gauntlet of this gang when they went out or returned home. We had arranged for our two elder children to go to local schools. Sarah had completed her first year at Stanground Comprehensive School, and now her second year of secondary education was to be at Richard Jefferies Junior High School, a short walk from where we lived. Actually, a big reorganisation of secondary education in the Swindon area was soon to be implemented; junior and senior high schools were to be amalgamated, and Sarah was later to go to the newly formed "Oakfield School", a little further away. Sixth form work was to be concentrated in Sixth Form Colleges; and in due course she was to transfer to "New College" (i.e. North-east Wiltshire College), occupying the site and buildings of the former Richard Jefferies School, together with those of an adjacent junior high school serving Walcot.

Michael still had one more year of primary education, and he went to Park North Junior School. Peter was later to go to Park North Infants and Junior Schools; and Michael transferred for secondary education to Churchfields School, a short way outside our parish, before he also joined New College. All of our children made good friends at their Swindon schools. Sarah also joined the "Thamesdown Singers" girls' choir, and widened her acquaintanceship considerably through that. We attended a number of excellent concerts that choir gave; and for several years they took a much appreciated part in the "Christingle Service" at St. John's Church at Christmas-time, held in aid of the Children's Society. Michael, who was already keen on conjuring before we moved to Swindon, had the good fortune to be introduced to the Wiltshire Association of Magicians. That group helped him on enormously. He began to give "magic shows" at children's parties, etc. from about the age of thirteen, and in due course was accepted into the Magic Circle. Paul Daniels was for some time Michael's hero. He met him on several occasions, and I remember attending Paul Daniels' shows at Oxford, Blackpool and the Savoy Theatre, London. Michael came to know a number of other young up-and-coming magicians, of both sexes, and we liked his "magic" friends very much.

I tried to use my first few months at Swindon as a time of getting to know the place and the people, and I quickly found some whom I liked very much. However, I did inherit a good deal of "baggage" from before my time, that did seem to weigh the church down. There were a number of unresolved conflicts and personality clashes, and at St. John's at least there did not appear to be any clear focus in mission to the surrounding population. Financial problems sapped morale, and it would not have been very helpful to say what is generally true, that financial problems are symptoms of deeper spiritual problems. Council estates are by their very nature not wealthy places, and there was a certain amount of very definite poverty.

I was alarmed by the large number of people there seemed to be who had left St. John's Church through disillusionment, as their only way of escaping from the bickering that they had found there, or because nobody seemed to listen to what they thought should be priorities in the church's agenda. Continuing vandalism of church property put a strain on some people's faith in God. There were some who from a strict church upbringing had very strong views about Christian discipline and correctness of liturgy; others felt that a much greater informality ought to be the order of the day, particularly for appealing to people with little or no church background, whom we wanted to attract.

I found very soon that the ecumenical "Mission Council", consisting of the ministerial team of St. John's and St. Andrew's Anglican Churches, Queens Drive Methodist Church, and Holy Family Roman Catholic Church, together with elected representatives of all those churches, was a body with a lot of potential. House groups were organised by the Mission Council, for Lent, and with some continuing throughout the year, and each group contained people of different denominations. Study days, courses of addresses, the Christian Aid house-to-house collection, Christmas hospitality and entertainment for down-and-outs (run jointly with a neighbouring Local Ecumenical Project) became part of the regular programme. A good number of joint services were held. The Methodist minister and I changed places on occasional Sundays.

The Roman Catholic church welcomed members of other churches to special services there and though we had to respect Roman Catholic rules about restricting the receiving of Communion there to members of the RC church, other Christians could receive a blessing at their altar; and the Roman Catholic priest, his curate, and many of their congregation came and received a blessing at the altar at St. John's Church on some occasions at Holy Communion. Social activities in the churches were made as far as possible open to all. A much valued Men's Fellowship was started as an ecumenical venture. I will explain in due course some very significant developments of the ecumenical dream, which came to pass in practice.

Having said all that, I have to admit that during much of the 1982-3 period, after my initial settling-in, for the next two years or so, I was not very happy at Swindon, and sometimes wondered whether I had made a mistake in going there. I questioned whether I was the right sort of person to be Rector in that type of parish – and wondered a bit why those who interviewed me did not seem to question it. Quite often people said to me, "Of course this isn't really the right place for you." The gulf between the Church and the community seemed immense. The Church did not seem to be very highly regarded by the community. The "community leaders" appeared to disregard the Church altogether, and would certainly not have thought of the clergy as co-leaders with them.

The "gang culture" was something that I had never really properly understood. I don't think I was very good at creating the right relationships with our local gang. Those boys didn't like me much. One big eye-opener for me was when I went into St. John's Church one day by the back door to do marriage registers. (The church was regrettably normally kept locked.) The boys rushed into the church, making a lot of noise, uttering obscenities; they picked up books and kneelers, and threw them around. They hid underneath the altar, got hold of candlesticks, upset the register ink, making a terrible mess; and I just wondered what they had ever been taught at home or school about what the Church stood for. Were they totally spiritually deprived? Was that a serious aspect of the "deprivation" that people associated with estates of that type? Or might they think, "What is God for me? What have I got to thank him for? Isn't the Church just a lot of meaningless mumbo-jumbo? Doesn't its bluff need to be called? And how better to call its bluff than to treat it with utter scorn and disrespect?" Very uncomfortable questions; but I felt forced to think about them, and profoundly challenged.

Things came to a very unpleasant head shortly after one or two older boys came along and joined forces with the boy who seemed to be the main leader of the gang. The older boys were constantly cheeky to me. One day, when I went out to do some work in our garden, I found one of the older boys sitting astride the gate into our driveway, and others pushing him back and forth, swinging the gate. They took no notice of my request that they should stop doing that. What they did notice, however, was that the gate was getting a bit loose – and it wouldn't take all that much effort to smash it down. With kicks and heaves they soon had the gate lying on the ground. I was of course furious, and that sent them into peals of laughter. It was just what they wanted – to see how far they could go. They then started playing football, and deliberately sending the ball into our garden. I returned it several times, and then said that they wouldn't get it back next time. That was what they hoped to hear, of course, and see what I would do. Within a few seconds the ball was in the garden again, and without saying anything I ran with it into the house and hid it. For a time I ignored their loud demands to have it back. Then, still holding the garden hoe in my hand, I went to get the ball and give it back to them. The vitriolic abuse that I got, particularly from the ringleader, led me to shake the hoe at him and tell him to go away and leave us alone. Quite exactly what happened is not entirely clear, as it was all so quick. I had not intended to hurt him; but in a split second I found my hoe handle in contact with that older boy's head.

To cut a long story short, I soon found myself at the police station, accused of assault. I didn't know whether the case would go to court. I immediately told the churchwardens, my ministerial colleagues, the Bishop of Malmesbury and the Archdeacon of Swindon. I had visions of being suspended from duty till the case was heard. I had fears of publicity in the local newspaper, publicity that would do harm to the Church. The future then seemed terribly uncertain. I didn't want our children to suffer. Anyhow, eventually, about six weeks later, I heard that I would get a police caution. Of course what had happened was all over our part of the estate in no time. Fortunately, little was said to our daughter at school. My ministry, dare I say the credibility of the Church, was very badly set back by that incident. I had to expect that members of the gang of boys would keep on reminding me of it when they saw me – and I was sometimes stopped in the street by other boys and girls whom I did not know, asking, "Are you the vicar who hit our friend?" As it was, we remained at Swindon for another eight years after the unforgettable date of 22 March 1982. Some people, who thought we would soon leave, did seem quite impressed that we were determined to put that nasty business behind us, and press on with the work that there was to be done, and into new developments of it.

It may be a bit of a relief now to turn to the transport aspects of where we were living. Our estates spread over a wide area, beginning about a mile and a half south-east from the centre of Swindon. Our railway station was Swindon, which was very well served by fast InterCity 125 trains from Paddington on both the Bristol and South Wales lines. The quickest trains were in London within fifty minutes. Bristol was reached in thirty-five minutes. There was a branch at Swindon for Gloucester, via Stroud. A few through trains ran to and from Paddington on that branch; but it was mostly served by diesel multiple unit trains which linked Swindon and Cheltenham at hourly intervals, with a few extended to Worcester. Later in our time the new "Sprinter" trains took over that route, and also introduced a few journeys a day to Westbury, on the London to the South-west main line, facilitating some connections. Many commuters travelled daily to Paddington from Swindon; and although we were in Bristol diocese, I always felt that Swindon looked much more to London than to Bristol.

The bus services in Swindon in general, and in our estates in particular, were excellent. Swindon was one of the decreasing number of towns where local public transport remained under the control of the local authority. What had been Swindon Corporation bus services were now called "Thamesdown Transport", since the local government changes of 1974. As well as very frequent buses to Swindon town centre from where we lived, there was also a useful "outer circle" service, reminiscent of Birmingham. That provided direct links to the hospital, to the new West Swindon development, to Coate Water Country Park, and other places where people might wish to go, without having to go into town and out again. By the time we lived there most Thamesdown buses were Fleetline rear-engined double-deckers. From 1982 for some years the policy was to acquire the new Dennis Dominator model.

Out-of-town buses, when we first got to Swindon, were those of the Bristol Omnibus Company, in National Bus Company leaf-green. Regular services were provided to Marlborough (now I saw that service from the other end of the route, compared with some thirty years earlier!); Calne; Chippenham; Malmesbury; Wootton Bassett (frequently); Cricklade, Cirencester and Cheltenham; Oxford (jointly with City of Oxford buses); Hungerford; and a number of villages. In 1983 the northern and eastern section of the Bristol company was hived off to a new "Cheltenham and Gloucester Omnibus Company", still part of NBC. The green buses serving Swindon were then painted red, and carried the fleetname "Swindon and District", as part of the Cheltenham and Gloucester Company's "local identity" policy. Bristol VR double-deckers and RE single-deckers, with some Leyland Nationals, formed most of the fleet. These were later added to by new Leyland Olympian double-deckers. The minibus flood that completely changed the bus scene in many parts of the country did not happen in Swindon. The frequently served town routes needed large vehicles to carry their passengers.

A few lighter Thamesdown routes were changed over to minibus operation; and some new links were provided where minibuses could use roads that were not suitable for full size buses. Swindon and District increased its half-hourly Swindon – Wroughton double-deck service to a ten minute frequency with the use of minibuses instead; the route was marketed under the name "Metro", as were a number of local services elsewhere in the Cheltenham and Gloucester company's area. The deregulation of local bus services in 1986 did not see significant service changes in Swindon. When Cheltenham and Gloucester (including Swindon & District) was privatised about 1987, some new and fairly striking liveries were introduced, in the same style but with different colours for the various parts of the company's operating area. Swindon and District took a dark shade of red for its main colour. Later, after I left, it became part of the Stagecoach empire.

No big group swallowed up Thamesdown, as it continued proudly to serve the citizens of Swindon. What did happen, I suppose in the interests of economical use of vehicles, was that when a reorganisation of some routes took place, Thamesdown and Swindon and District worked jointly (rather in Southend style) on several services which went to outlying housing areas on the fringe of the expanding Swindon built-up area.

Back to parish work – and in July 1983 the Revd Stephen Bessent relinquished his post as team vicar with charge of St. Andrew's, Walcot, and moved to Middlesbrough. That was a serious loss to us. Many had very greatly valued his ministry; and I personally had gained much through working with him. It meant that I was for a time the only Anglican priest on the staff; and though Olive, our woman worker, was extremely energetic and useful, I had to take much more part in the life of St. Andrew's, particularly for Holy Communion there. Also there was the matter of the appointment of a suitable priest to be Stephen's successor.

Without going into much detail, and trying not to say anything unfair, I was greatly concerned that there was an element of division over policy matters at St. Andrew's that rather came to a head after Stephen moved away. Some people there got very angry with me for "taking the bull by the horns". I didn't want the next team vicar to come and find the dispute unresolved. It all ultimately related to the place of women in the church's ministry. We had Olive there, doing excellent work – and also a woman training for licensing as a Reader. Had people in the congregation the right to try to prevent these women from administering the chalice at Holy Communion? The Archdeacon said emphatically that those authorised for any kind of ministry must be permitted to exercise it. The problem delayed the appointment of a new team vicar. While consideration was given to the idea of advertising (as for Farcet), the Archdeacon of Swindon, who was by then the Ven. Kenneth Clark (in my view an outstandingly good and caring archdeacon) suggested to me the name of a priest who he thought would be very suitable, and who was looking for a new post. He was the Revd Bill Clynes, already in Bristol diocese. Bill had had a Methodist background, and had been involved in the Bristol City Mission.

When he and his wife Margaret came to visit us, I felt he was just what was wanted. I felt much pleasure and relief when Bill was licensed as team vicar on Advent Sunday, 1983. He certainly had a gift of getting on with people, and under his influence the divisive problems at St. Andrew's largely died down. I remember him saying to me once that if you have to walk on eggshells, it is impossible to do so without breaking some of them. I was also able to concentrate more on St. John's and the Park North and Park South estates which it served.

To change the subject again to our family life and developments, Priscilla and I tried to give our children good and interesting holidays. Up until 1983 we generally used to go to British seaside resorts for our main summer holiday. In 1984 for the first time we went abroad together as a family, flying from Heathrow to

Geneva, and staying at Montreux, in a beautiful lakeside setting. We explored some Swiss mountain resorts, seeing them look a bit different, of course, in summer, from how they would have appeared in winter; but there was skiing going on in August at Les Diablerets, where we went one day. Sarah, in particular, could not get over the beauty of the area surrounding Gstaad, which we reached by a magnificent mountain railway.

The Swiss trains are renowned for their efficiency and the impressive routes they take. The cross-channel ferry referred to in the title of this chapter is that between Dover and Ostend. We had booked to travel on it in August 1985; and on the previous evening, when seeing the television weather forecast, the presenter started by saying something I had never heard before, and never have since: "Anyone crossing the Channel tomorrow will be in for a rough time." When we boarded the ferry at Dover, it seemed badly overcrowded; the reason was that the hydrofoils had all been cancelled that day because of the rough conditions.

Anyhow, by about halfway across, the winds eased a good deal, and the latter part of the voyage was quite pleasant, if breezy. We stayed at Ostend, with its seaside amenities, and from there visited Bruges and Brussels by train, and other places around by tram and coach. I have never taken our car or hired a car overseas. So people who go abroad with me have to put up with my interest in sampling the public transport available.

In 1986 we did hire a car, because we stayed in the left-hand drive United Kingdom. We flew from Heathrow to Inverness, picked up our car, and stayed for nine days at Fort Augustus, on Loch Ness; it made a very good centre for trips in all directions, including a day on the Isle of Skye. We also tried to get in as much walking as was acceptable to the family. Michael, with his interest in magic, was fascinated by the Loch Ness Monster, and the Visitors' Centre devoted to that subject at Drumnadrochet.

The next year we were back in the Alps, this time at Chamonix, at the foot of Mont Blanc. We were amazed and enthralled by the network of cable car routes existing in that area, going right up well beyond the snow line. Our time there included a lovely railway journey to Annecy, with its beautiful lake. 1988 saw us in Germany, with Rover tickets on the German railways. We stayed at Kirchzarten, near Freiburg, in Black Forest country. Trains took us to Basle (just over the Swiss border), the impressive lakes at Titisee and Schluchsee, Europa Park, a superb theme park on the German/French border, Freiburg itself (it seemed a bit funny having lunch at McDonald's there, much the same as McDonald's in Swindon – or anywhere!), and a village station from which we were able to do a superb walk in the Black Forest. Guide books and tourist leaflets in that part of the world we found to be really excellent, and available in English.

The next year we followed up our son Peter's strong desire to go to Denmark's Legoland, which he had seen on television. We stayed quite near Billund, where Legoland is, at a town called Veijle. It is not really a holiday resort, but has pleasant surroundings, and the great advantage of being on the intercity railway line. So from there we went by train to Aarhus, with its fascinating open-air museum, to Odense, with its Hans Christian Andersen associations, and (to me) very interesting transport museum, and of course to Copenhagen.

At that time it was necessary to do part of the journey from Jutland by ferry, the train running through on the ferry. On our outward journey we could rejoin the train at a station adjacent to where the ferry landed. However, on the return journey, having left the train at that station to board the boat, we assumed that we would be able to get back into the train where we had left in the morning at a station on the quay. Some announcements were made in Danish shortly before the ferry tied up. Without our realising it, they were instructing passengers to re-board the train in the depths of the ship.

On arrival, we went down a gangway on to dry land as did a considerable number of other passengers – but they weren't intending to go on the train; they had parked their cars, which they were going to pick up. To our horror we saw the train come off the ship, and not stop till it had reached a station platform a quarter of a mile or so further on. An official said that if we hurried along the railway line we should be able to catch it; and he phoned the station where the train was waiting to request the train to wait until we got to it. We had to pick our steps very carefully, and it was beginning to get dark. Sarah unfortunately slipped, and got up covered in black grime.

Keep Me Travelling

What a relief it was when we reached the train. A split second after we had boarded the train set off to take us back to Veijle. That was not an experience any of us are very likely to forget. Peter was by then aged ten, so he could cope all right with the "railway walk"; it would have been much more difficult with a younger child.

After Easter each year we used to go away with Priscilla's father for a short break before the school term started. He was (and is, now in his nineties) a very keen walker, with a fondness for revisiting places he knew in his younger days. Several times we went to Exmoor, where he had taken parties of boys from Highgate School for walking holidays; I renewed my acquaintance with Dunster, with vivid memories of 1941 still clear in my mind – I could have walked round the village blindfold! At different times we went with him to the South Downs (full of boyhood memories for him), Dartmoor, the Malvern hills, the Brecon Beacons, Cornwall (Priscilla's father was particularly fond of the Lizard area, with memories of visits there when he was young), the Isle of Wight, and Dovedale and the Peak District.

Of course the country around Swindon was magnificent, with the Wiltshire Downs so close, and the Cotswolds in the other direction. We became familiar with the M4, which enabled us to get easily to my mother at Bristol. After a few years, however, she moved to a flat at Poole, Dorset, to be close to my brother William. We could still quite easily visit her there before her death.

In 1985 Bristol diocese was experimenting with the idea of appointing "Parish Coordinators" to the ministerial staff of some of the town parishes, particularly urban priority areas. Their task was to build bridges between the church and the community in which it was set, and try to discern and implement ways in which the church could serve the community's needs more effectively.

Mr Richard Hyde (who at the time was just completing his training to be a Licensed Reader) was appointed to serve Parks and Walcot parish as Coordinator. He made a big difference, and we had reason to be very grateful to him. He made detailed investigations into the needs of children in the area, and managed to organise an excellent summer holiday club, attended by many children who had no previous contact with the church. That lasted for several days with indoor and outdoor activities. He was the inspiration too behind the establishment of an after-school playscheme, which attracted quite good numbers, and enabled us to get to know many more families. Richard succeeded in finding just the right people to help to run these ventures, and he was very good at getting funding for them.

We even managed to take the playscheme children to the pantomime at a Swindon theatre, at no cost to their parents. The Social Responsibility officers of Bristol diocese were very helpful. Richard also took some very important preliminary steps before he left us towards the extensive improvement and re-equipment of St. John's church hall. As a result of that, it was possible to make the hall into an "Open House", where people could drop in, make and meet friends, have snacks – in fact pretty good lunches were on offer on certain days of the week – sit in comfort to read magazines that were available, watch television and videos, and altogether feel at home. The staffing of the Open House was possible because we could draw upon members of the Methodist and Roman Catholic churches in our group as well as the Church of England. The whole thing was seen as a united project. Certainly it was very much appreciated. The situation of St. John's Church, right at the heart of the Parks, just across the road from the main Cavendish Square shopping centre, was a great help. Shoppers could easily "drop in". We were very fortunate with the people who took main responsibility for the organisation of it all.

The ministry at Swindon was demanding, and, I think, fulfilling. Two women were licensed as Readers while I was there, and both took a very useful part in sharing in the leading of worship and associated pastoral care. I should perhaps have mentioned that Richard Hyde's coming was in a sense in place of Olive, our pastoral worker, when she retired. We did unfortunately have big problems with the structure of St. John's Church. A certain type of concrete had been used in its construction, which did not stand the test of time. The impressive tower, a landmark on the estate, was declared to be unsafe. I felt all the more uncomfortable when strong winds blew up.

Eventually, the tower had to be taken down, to many people's horror – and what caused particular annoyance was the way that so much rubble from the demolition, together with the impressive cross that had surmounted the tower, was left lying about for a considerable time. One local resident said, "They're taking a long time to pull the rest of the church down!" When the work was completed, the cross was re-erected at ground level near the main door; and a completely new and attractive entrance was constructed. However, the building didn't look right – its proportions seemed incorrect – without the tower.

A dreadful story now – but it is the sort of thing that one has to be prepared for in ministry in areas of deprivation, and where children are not well disciplined. The Sunday School leader was driven to distraction by the behaviour of a nine-year-old boy. In fact other children were leaving the Sunday School because he caused such annoyance and disruption. Eventually the superintendent asked me if I would go round to see the boy's parents and request them not to send the boy to Sunday School for the time being. That was the sort of job that I did not like to have to do at all; and I put it off for a few days, until by the Thursday of the week I thought I'd better go.

I didn't always buy an evening newspaper, but on that Thursday afternoon when I was in a newsagent's I caught sight of the paper's main headlines, "Chicken Boy Tragedy". I wondered what that meant, and bought the paper. On reading it I found that a boy had been killed by a car when playing "chicken" with friends on the main road through our estate, and that boy was the very one whose parents I was planning to see about his behaviour at Sunday School. You can imagine the shock I got, and how thankful I was that I had gone into that newsagent's shop. When I visited the family, I did so for a very different reason from what I had originally expected. The boy's funeral was quite a big occasion; and a Children's Bible was given to the Sunday School in his memory.

When we were at Swindon our daughter Sarah started a teacher training course at Bishop Grosseteste College, Lincoln, incorporating degree work in English at Hull University. Michael went to read Geography at Leicester University. On one occasion, en route to Leicester, we stopped at Banbury for refreshments and a walk around the town – little realising how well we would come to know the place in the future! My licence at Swindon was for ten years. We actually stayed there for nine.

Thanks to the excellent "clearing-house" system for clergy appointments, by which my name was circulated to bishops and patrons as one seeking a new post, I received a letter from the Bishop of Derby, the Right Revd Peter Dawes, whom I had known very slightly when he was a vicar in Chelmsford diocese (in fact some boys from his church choir had joined a choir holiday school led by our Chigwell daughter-church choirmaster in Dorset, in which I had taken part, in 1961). Knowing that I was a team rector in an ecumenical situation, he wondered whether I would be interested in being considered for the team rectorship of a new grouping of parishes near Chesterfield. The church for which I would be primarily responsible would be St. Lawrence's, North Wingfield. There would be five other churches in the group, with a ministerial team serving them. Rather as with Swindon, I paid a preliminary visit on my own, and was struck by the very warm welcome I received.

Then Priscilla and I both had to go to be more formally interviewed. It was a bit of a formidable gathering, with clergy and some of the churchwardens; two of the existing clergy in the team I had not met on my previous visit, because they had been away. I sensed a very big division there; it was clear that in one of the churches a charismatic evangelical worship style had been introduced – and the priest who was in charge of that church asked me some pointed questions, obviously designed to see how sympathetic I was to the evangelical standpoint and policies.

It did not really surprise me when the Bishop wrote back to me to say that that team vicar and his churchwardens were not happy about the prospect of my appointment, but the others all were. The Bishop asked me to meet with him at Derby to discuss the situation. I really wondered whether I ought to drop further consideration of the appointment; but the Bishop did not think the objections that he had received to my going there were too serious, and he believed that we could probably patch things up with a bit of Christian goodwill. That was what I tried to do by very carefully worded letters to those who had expressed such strong reservations about my appointment. The result was that the Bishop felt all was now well. So did I more or less.

My appointment was made official. It was not until I got to North Wingfield that I realised what a lot of unfinished business there still was over the whole concept of this new team parish. Our time there will be described in the next chapter.

We left Swindon with happy memories far outweighing the unhappy ones. I have not so far explained the changes in the Bristol diocesan hierarchy that took place in the years when we were in the diocese. Bishop John Tinsley, who was extremely nice when I did see him, but with whom I had little contact, retired from being Bishop of Bristol in 1985; and in his place came Bishop Barry Rogerson (with whom I had had slight earlier contact). Both he and the much-loved Bishop Freddy Temple's successor as Bishop of Malmesbury, the Right Revd Peter Firth, could not have been more supportive of the work at Parks and Walcot and of my own ministry in particular. Nor could Kenneth Clark, Archdeacon of Swindon, whom I have already mentioned, and the Bristol Diocesan Board of Social Responsibility. I had sometimes heard clergy in some dioceses complain that their "fathers-in-God" took no interest in them. I can truthfully say that I have never had that feeling.

CHAPTER 9

Horses; Troublesome drives via Syresham; Introduction to the Stagecoach Empire; "Super-Sprinters".

Before saying anything else about North Wingfield, I would like to point out here that Priscilla and I and our family have many very happy memories of our seven years there, and good friends from that time. However, as I said at the end of the last chapter, I arrived at a time when the "unfinished business" regarding the new team ministry arrangements caused rather a lot of conflicts. I had great respect for all my colleagues in the ministry there, but I am not going to mention any of their names, for fear of seeming at all unfair. I can truthfully say that all were very conscientious and sincere in their beliefs. There was never a case of any not pulling their weight, which I know can cause problems in some team ministries. The Archdeacon said that our six-church parish was a "microcosm" of the Church of England. Generally churches and clergy of differing ecclesiastical outlooks can get on and pursue their own policies regardless of the policies that other churches in their locality may pursue.

However, if our team ministry was to mean anything, and the united parish be a reality, it was of course necessary to formulate clear principles and rules. One Parochial Church Council served the whole parish, with members from all the churches. Each church had its own District Church Council, to which certain matters were delegated, particularly regarding its own finances, care of its own buildings, and the forms of its regular services. The Parochial Church Council, fed with ideas from the ministerial team meetings, set the boundaries within which each local church should work as part of the whole set-up. If different pastoral policies (for instance regarding baptism, marriage of divorced people, etc.) were followed by different clergy and churches, big problems could arise – yet each team vicar had the rights and responsibilities of an incumbent.

So there was a delicate balancing act to keep going. I said earlier that I did not see myself as belonging to any "party" within the Church of England – I could see positive things and helpful insights in all parties. All the clergy with whom I had hitherto worked were somewhere around the central tradition of churchmanship. My last real contact with Evangelicals had been my short-lived initial association with the CICCU at Cambridge. What became very evident to me in North Wingfield parish was the desire of some of the Evangelical people of the parish to make the whole parish take the Evangelical stance, and the strong resistance to that from church members of a rather more high-church or liberal tradition.

In certain circles I was not really acceptable as the first Team Rector of this new set-up. Tensions arose over such things as the propriety of having raffles at fund-raising events; that caused quite a storm. It was very necessary to find where we could "agree to differ" without jeopardising the unity, fellowship and co-operation on which the uniting of separate parishes into one was built. We were enormously helped by Canon Tony Chesterman, who became our team consultant. We met with him for a day several times a year; and thereby I think we learned better to understand each other's point of view, and respect each other's deeply held convictions, thus greatly facilitating our working together.

The six churches were as follows: St. Lawrence's church, North Wingfield, a very beautiful medieval church, was the "mother church" of the whole area, very prominent at the top of a hill – "the draughtiest corner of Derbyshire" in the words of a former archdeacon. North Wingfield was an old village settlement, which had grown and spread enormously, and now consisted largely of housing estates which looked to Chesterfield, four or five miles away, as their main centre. For the previous century or more, North Wingfield had been right in the middle of an extensive coal mining area; but all the pits had closed by the time we came to the parish. There were many former miners living in the community. North Wingfield parish church had a tradition of fairly traditional central churchmanship.

My predecessor as Rector had done a lot of work towards the formation of the team ministry and united parish; indeed it existed in embryo during his time; a combined parish magazine had been in existence for a few years. I was led to think that a major reason for my predecessor leaving after only three years or so was his frustration at the slowness of decision making about this new set-up, his fearing at several times that it would never get off the ground at all, and the complex legal processes that seemed to slow everything up. It was no secret that there had been considerable opposition to the scheme among some people at North Wingfield – and I did meet with some bitterness from some former long-standing church members, who felt they could only show their anger at not being properly consulted by dropping out of church life altogether. North Wingfield had a hundred-year-old daughter-church – St. John's at Tupton. This was situated in New Tupton, a mile and a half from St. Lawrence's, and served a rather, straggly semi-built-up area consisting of a wide range of types of housing. St. John's always seemed to me to be a bit more "jolly" than St. Lawrence's, less inhibited, perhaps.

The very able team vicar who was there when we arrived moved on after a few years – his fairly "gentle" evangelicalism seemed to accommodate quite easily people of that persuasion as well as some of a more traditional Anglican stance. When he left, a new team vicar was appointed to have primary charge of St. John's. He made a very favourable impression very quickly; but after less than a year he was "redeployed" within the team, to take charge of St. Bartholomew's, Clay Cross, as I shall shortly describe. When that happened, St. John's got a woman priest as team vicar. She had actually come to North Wingfield some fourteen years before as a deaconess, had in the mean time been ordained deacon, and then in 1994 priest, among the first women priests in the diocese. She had become very much loved at North Wingfield (among churchgoers and non-churchgoers alike) through her conscientious pastoral work; her preaching and conduct of worship were also much appreciated. She was in great demand for taking funerals, and deservedly so in view of the trouble she took. She had always been anxious to maintain the ethos of St. Lawrence's that made those who were sensitive to catholic tradition feel comfortable.

Her moving to Tupton greatly displeased many North Wingfield people; but now that she was a priest it seemed the obvious thing; the diocese was not offering us a new member of staff to replace the latest team vicar to have left. I got a bit of flak for transferring her away from North Wingfield, and a few, I think, never forgave me for it. She had some "withdrawal symptoms" herself – and neither she nor I had anticipated the difficulties she would face from a few at St. John's who were of a strong evangelical persuasion. Her subsequent work at St. John's was valued by many, and she was left in peace when a few people changed their allegiance within the parish to a church that was suited to their style.

St. Bartholomew's, Clay Cross, retained its parish church status within the new parish of North Wingfield. Clay Cross had been a small colliery town, and was a local shopping centre for the surrounding districts. The team vicar whom I found "in situ" had during the last six years enlivened the church considerably by introducing a far more definite evangelical stance. A fair number of new people had joined the church, who previously did not attend worship anywhere, and who would say that they had come to know the Lord Jesus Christ through the ministry and outreach of St. Bartholomew's. Inevitably changes in any church are going to alienate some people, but those who felt that the new style St. Bartholomew's was not their cup of tea were outnumbered by those who had come newly into the church's life. In that perspective perhaps it is understandable that suspicions should be aroused if a new Team Rector should be appointed who was not of the evangelical school of thought. It is not for me to make judgements.

The strength of evangelical churches may owe something to the authority that their clergy sometimes claim. There were fundamental differences between this team vicar and myself over doctrinal and pastoral matters. However, I think we co-operated where we could; and he was generous enough to accept my position of responsibility within the parish as a whole. When he left, to serve in Morocco with the Inter-Continental Church Society, the team vicar from Tupton took his place, and that appointment was widely welcomed.

The existing music group at St. Bartholomew's continued, together with the informal "celebration" services held twice a month on Sunday evenings, and the twice-monthly family services on Sunday mornings, at which the music group played choruses and modern-style hymns. On other Sundays there was Holy Communion as the Sunday morning service, with the organ providing music which was on the whole more traditional. Exchanges of ministers on certain Sundays meant that I officiated from time to time at St. Bartholomew's and all the other churches. There were two daughter-churches belonging to the former Clay Cross parish. One of them, St. Barnabas', Danesmoor, served a former mining community, with quite a bit of other industry in it, contiguous to Clay Cross. The other, St. Mark's, Handley, was in a very rural setting, in the beautiful countryside bordering on the Peak District.

Two very small communities, Handley and Woolley Moor, were served by St. Mark's church, and there was a Church of England (controlled) primary school. For my first year or so there was a priest who was technically curate, having primary charge of the Danesmoor and Handley churches. He was much missed when he moved to become vicar of a parish not far away – and the rest of us shared Danesmoor and Handley between us for a time, until the woman priest at Tupton took on Handley as well, and I took main responsibility for Danesmoor. It was a struggling church, but it had the advantage of a very warm and friendly worshipping community, making me feel very welcome.

The other main element of the parish was Pilsley, with its own parish church. Some years before I came it had been made into a team ministry with North Wingfield and Tupton, and there were those who thought that was a big enough grouping without the addition of the three churches of Clay Cross parish. Pilsley was geographically a bit out on a limb, looking more towards Alfreton than Chesterfield; and it stretched a long way with housing in ribbon development along the road that led to North Wingfield. Pilsley had also had its local coal mines – and I must say how very well the areas that had been covered with mines had been landscaped since their closure; pleasant walking routes, "pit trails", as they were called, followed the old tracks of the pit railways. There was a vacancy in the team vicarship at Pilsley when I first came; and so I was quite heavily involved there for a time. The appointment of a new team vicar was a priority; and St. Mary's Church, Pilsley, and the community it served were given an extremely gifted young man to be their spiritual leader. Pilsley already had a tradition of being rather on the evangelical side; their new team vicar placed it most firmly in the evangelical camp. I learned a lot from him, not least about communication – and he seemed to encourage people to come to church on the grounds that what they would find there would be very different from their expectations or their previous experience of church worship and life. It was different, most certainly – particularly the "Good News at Ten" service held on two Sunday mornings a month. No one could possibly be bored!

A drama group played a much valued part in many services, and a music group was formed, as at Clay Cross. Most certainly there were people in the community who joined the church for the first time under this new regime, and who quickly became committed Christians. Some people from other parts of the parish, and from further afield, started going regularly to Pilsley church. Different people had, and have, different tastes in worship – you can say that our parish as a whole tried to cater for those different tastes, though those wanting high Anglo-Catholic services would have to look elsewhere.

When there was a fifth Sunday in the month, we used to have a Team Service in the evening at one of our churches. Rather than trying to work out some mishmash of different styles, we tried to arrange it so that the traditions and styles of whichever church was the venue for the service were adhered to. I told people that the team services were occasions when we must all forget our personal preferences. However, for some people that was difficult. Team services often seemed to bring a crop of complaints and grumbles, mainly about the music; and it was not easy to persuade some people to support them at all. However, they were supposed to be an expression of our fellowship in the one parish.

I had not previously realised how strongly many evangelicals disliked traditional-style Anglican worship, with the old hymns, and the form of Prayer Book Evensong, with its psalms, canticles, and sung responses. Others, mainly older people, loved it, and found in it a beauty that they greatly valued. At one team service, at Pilsley, a visiting preacher introduced the "Toronto Blessing", seen as a re-enactment of the worshipping experience of the early Christians in Biblical times, filled with the Holy Spirit. The effect was dynamic. The church became littered with people lying on the floor, making what seemed strange noises, overwhelmed by a sense of release by God from a whole range of emotional hangups and from some physical troubles from which they had suffered. Not having that experience myself rather disqualifies me from commenting on what actually happened; but you will realise that many were aware of an enormously strong spiritual power. That was what regular worshippers at Pilsley (and also, I think, Clay Cross) were frequently discovering when they met together in Christ's name.

However, to those who had no such expectation, the whole thing was most distasteful. I was begged to ensure that no future team services should include anything like it. In fact I was criticised by some for allowing it on that one occasion. It was something of a watershed in my ministry as team rector. I was clearly having to come to terms with there being a strong polarisation of attitudes in the parish, and to try to find the best ways of handling that.

This next bit is difficult and painful to write. The period around 1995-6 I did not find at all satisfactory. It was quite evident that my supposed leadership of the team was by now really in name only. The real strength and vitality was in the two evangelical churches in the parish, Clay Cross and Pilsley. Morale had sunk pretty low in North Wingfield church, which seemed to be stagnating, while Clay Cross and Pilsley were going great guns. I was under pressure from some North Wingfield people to liven up St. Lawrence's Church; while others did not want St. Lawrence's to lose its tradition of having quieter, more meditative services. Two or three open meetings were held to allow people to express their concerns and wishes publicly (it was only really the "innovators" who attended these meetings) –

and when ideas that had come out of the meetings were brought to the District Church Council, they were readily accepted. On two Sunday mornings a month, and two Sunday evenings we had more informal styles of worship, being careful to use authorised material from some new publications; and we sang some of the more modern hymns from the Mission Praise book, which the PCC agreed to purchase. On the other Sundays we had the Alternative Service Book Holy Communion in the morning, and Prayer Book Evensong.

That was an attempt to accommodate everyone – but it didn't really work. The more "dyed in the wool" churchgoers resented changes of that nature; those who were after something more exciting for modern times to attract outsiders felt that the more informal services were still far too low key. There wasn't the ebullience and enthusiasm that were so evident elsewhere in the parish. The organist cooperated most loyally, though his preference for the more traditional forms was no secret. The choir, such as it was, having got rather depleted over the years, was on the whole opposed to the introduction of the lighter-style hymns and choruses. In fact this spelt the beginning of the end for the choir, which disbanded within the next year or so.

The evangelical churches did not have choirs, and said they didn't need them because of the keen congregational singing. I tried tremendously hard, with the help of our two excellent Licensed Readers, to get things right. We couldn't possibly ape Clay Cross and Pilsley – nor would I have wished to; I got a lot of support and encouragement from some who felt we were on the right track; and by 1997 there were some new people coming quite regularly to the services. The effort put into a special Festival Weekend at North Wingfield in the summer of 1997, with displays of arts and crafts, as well as flowers, a very good concert by Dronfield church choir; and Sunday Evensong sung by the choir of Derby Cathedral boosted morale somewhat. By then, however, our time at North Wingfield was drawing to a close. My seven-year licence was soon to expire, and I certainly did not think it would be right to apply for an extension of it.

Perhaps I should add that during 1995 and 1996 I was involved in some rather unpleasant conflicts within the parish and community, which wore me down somewhat. I think the churchwardens were a bit concerned for my health. Gossip didn't help; and I was accused of saying things that I had never said. A storm blew up when some work was done in North Wingfield churchyard to bring the extensive ashes plot more into line with diocesan regulations. We notified the bereaved families who were affected of what was going to be done – but when it happened it gave some of them a much bigger shock than they were prepared for.

Maybe we had turned a blind eye for too long to what some families were doing to embellish their loved ones' plots in ways that were not in keeping with diocesan policy and the general feel of the churchyard. Some aggrieved people got the local newspaper to send a reporter and photographer without my prior knowledge – and the reporter rang me up, asking such questions as,

"Don't you think you've handled this business very insensitively?" Anyhow my unrehearsed answers to his questions, and reports of what I had earlier said to relatives of people whose ashes were buried, came out in the newspaper unfairly, I must say, in such a way as to turn the public's sympathies entirely to the bereaved people, and make me and the church out to be uncaring and discourteous.

For quite a time I had unpleasant things said to me by local people who never came to church; perhaps I gave some shorter shrift than I should have done, if I knew that their bereavement had been a good time ago. Someone whom I didn't know at all wrote to the Bishop of Derby on the strength of the piece in the paper. A local funeral director berated me well and truly, told me that I was extremely unpopular, and that his clients were asking not to have me to take the funerals of members of their families.

I don't think things ever got quite properly patched up between me and the funeral director. A step backward occurred when by some error of communication I didn't know about a cremation that I was supposed to be taking at Chesterfield until that undertaker rang me up half an hour before the service, concerned that I had made no contact with the family (but neither had the family made any contact with me!). So I had to take the service with total ignorance about the deceased – and the family would not receive me when later that day I went to apologise to them for the misunderstanding. They were bitterly angry, and did not reply to the letter I subsequently wrote to them.

I mention these things because they highlight the effects that some errors can have, and the importance of putting into writing anything that one may be asked to say to a newspaper reporter. You will understand if the funeral director's remarks knocked my confidence a bit at a time when I was already trying not very successfully to handle difficult issues of relationships within the parish.

To get now on to the transport arrangements around our Derbyshire parish, the two main railway lines southwards from Chesterfield, to Derby and Nottingham, both passed through the parish, though the nearest station was Chesterfield. There had been a Clay Cross station on both lines, close to where they forked, but that had been closed in the Beeching era. The Derby route went into a tunnel which passed under the centre of Clay Cross. From Chesterfield station there was an hourly service on the Sheffield to London St. Pancras line, served by InterCity 125 trains when we were there; London could be reached in about two and a quarter hours.

The long distance cross-country intercity services from the south-west of England or the south coast to north-east England and Scotland, via Birmingham, served Chesterfield, though not all trains stopped there. These are now part of "Virgin Cross-Country." There was also a long route served by express Super-Sprinter diesel multiple-unit trains, linking Liverpool with Norwich, running every hour, via Manchester, Sheffield, Chesterfield, Nottingham, and Peterborough. Between them these services provided about three trains an hour between Chesterfield and Sheffield, the journey taking only a quarter of an hour. Chesterfield, as you can see, was a good railway centre.

Local bus services were good too. The former Chesterfield Corporation Transport had been privatised; and its attractive blue and yellow buses served all parts of the town and its vicinity, including North Wingfield and Clay Cross. The East Midland Motor Services, running longer routes from Chesterfield, and serving much of north Derbyshire and Nottinghamshire, was taken over by the Stagecoach group.

During the latter part of our time Stagecoach swallowed up Chesterfield Transport; and its blue and yellow buses took the white and stripy Stagecoach livery, in which some of them looked odd. Some "rationalisation" of services followed; but North Wingfield retained its service every fifteen minutes to Clay Cross in one direction and Chesterfield in the other. Double and single-deck buses seemed to be completely interchangeable on this and many other routes. Trent buses also came through North Wingfield from points south; it was possible to reach Derby, Nottingham, Mansfield and Alfreton by regular Trent buses from North Wingfield; but it did take a long time to get to the more distant destinations; and for Derby and Nottingham it was certainly quicker to go into Chesterfield and get the train. Trent began to introduce smaller-capacity buses on some of its inter-urban routes, as passenger numbers fell.

A cryptic reference in the title of this chapter had better be explained here. When we moved from Swindon to North Wingfield, we had an Austin Montego car, which gave us good service. On our return journey to Swindon after our North Wingfield interview, the temperature gauge in the car suddenly shot up high, with the warning light flashing, as we passed through a village called Syresham, in Northamptonshire. An AA man came, and couldn't see any reason why that should have happened. He suggested we followed his car for a bit of way, and flashed our headlights if it happened again. It didn't, and we got home all right, if a bit delayed.

Some five months later, on the very day that we left Swindon, and were en route for North Wingfield, to move in, we were passing through Syresham again – and what should happen, but the temperature gauge again did exactly the same thing. It had not happened since our previous drive through Syresham. What an amazing coincidence – or was there some sinister secret about Syresham? I investigated carefully; and after leaving the car a bit of time to cool down, we proceeded on our journey, and had no further trouble. A little over a year later, Priscilla and I had reason to drive to Bristol – and as we were leaving the city on our return journey the same overheating warning came on, for a third time. There was a garage nearby; and I asked if they would examine the car. The man in charge said, "Oh no, it's not necessary to do that. Just drive on. The temperature gauge in Montego cars is always playing up!" So I knew that if it happened again, I needn't worry. I hoped the AA man who had come to our rescue at Syresham had by then discovered the truth!

But here is another coincidence – or don't our cars like us taking up new homes? The excellent Vauxhall Cavalier that we had when we eventually left North Wingfield for Oxfordshire (as I will explain in due course) made its strong protest when we had gone only a short way down the M1 on our moving day. Our son Peter sitting next to me suddenly said, "There's smoke." I had already noticed a rather funny smell, and when I looked down, there was some smoke coming from behind the steering wheel. We had our dog and three cats aboard the car, and Priscilla was sitting in the back. I hastily drove on to the hard shoulder, and when I switched off the engine, the smoke thankfully stopped.

The AA were very quick when I told them of our circumstances that day; and their engineer had to "hot-wire" the car to enable us to continue on our journey. The ignition switch had to be isolated – that's where the trouble was. By putting luminous paint at the ends of the two wires which had to be put in contact with each other to start the car, the AA man helped me to proceed in the dark. We had a new ignition switch fitted a few days later – but I was very glad that that mishap had occurred on the motorway, with its emergency telephones, rather than on some country road during hours of darkness.

Mention of Horses in the chapter title will need some explanation. I had never ridden, until 1992, though Priscilla had been a keen rider when she was a girl. In the summer of 1992, Priscilla, Peter (aged 13) and I went to an unusual destination for our summer holiday, namely Iceland. An aunt of mine used to stay there, and had said

Keep Me Travelling

that it was a place that we ought to try to get to one day. We had a marvellous time there, based on the capital, Rejkyavik; we visited some of the hot springs, and the impressive waterfalls. We had a lovely ferry trip to Akranes, saw small isolated villages, and wondered what it would be like to live there, particularly in the winter, with such terribly short hours of daylight.

When we were there in the summer, it hardly got dark at all. Brochures and guide books all seemed to recommend very strongly taking an excursion on horseback, to places well off the roads where the scenery was outstanding. There was a prominent advertisement for this in our hotel, saying, "No riding experience necessary." I made a few further inquiries, trying to make quite sure that novices would be safe and not at any serious disadvantage. So we went – and it was an exhilarating experience. The horses knew every inch of the route, and carried us along with little effort required on our part. After we got back to Derbyshire, I noticed in the local paper an advertisement for pony-trekking in the Peak District, again with no prior experience of riding being necessary. So one day Priscilla and I, this time accompanied by our daughter Sarah, took the plunge. We rode on a most scenic route, well away from roads – but we did have to ride on a fairly busy road at the beginning and end, which made me a bit uneasy. The horse I had was rather lazy, unlike my Icelandic horse, and the leader of the ride shouted, "Kick him hard!"

Priscilla was keen, a bit more so than I was, to go again on another day a few weeks later. This time my horse (a different one) kept on wanting to eat grass – and I think he sensed that I was not really in full control of him. The cure-all for all ills again seemed to be the instruction to kick powerfully – it was recommended to wear walking-boots if you didn't possess riding-boots. After that I felt that if we were to go trekking again it would be wise to have a few riding lessons. We went to stables near where we lived; and it was soon very clear that a gulf separated the attitudes of trekking centres and riding schools.

We learned that riding was all about getting the perfect rapport between horse and rider, learning to use your legs primarily, with the help of your hands and your seat, to give the horse sensitive guidance and impulsion, so that it would willingly go where you wanted it to go, at the speed and pace of the rider's choice. The riding-school horses were much more responsive than the trekking centre horses. Successful riding certainly wasn't a matter of trying to overcome a horse's laziness and self-will by slamming your boots into its sides with all your strength – even if that was what it had seemed like to me when we had gone trekking. We did keep up having riding lessons, and went for some local hacks. It was a good way of keeping fit. We also invested in the right garb. The next time we ventured on a Peak District trek, with a friend who was keen to go with us, I felt much more confident, and I think that communicated itself to the horse!

I won't detail all the holidays we had from North Wingfield. Particularly memorable was a trip to the Holy

Land that Priscilla's father gave us as a present to mark our Silver Wedding in 1993. Two years later we had a few days in Paris after Easter, with Peter. Priscilla's father, then aged eighty-five, travelled over for the day by Eurostar on one of the days we were there. We met him at the Gare du Nord in mid-morning, had a good time with him during the day, saw him off in the early evening; and he was back at his home in Highgate, North London, in time, if not for an early night, at any rate not a late one! We had flown to Paris from East Midlands Airport, very conveniently placed for us.

Our younger son Peter started secondary education when we got to North Wingfield – at Tupton Hall School, which had an excellent reputation; and his career there exactly spanned our time in the parish. It was important that we should bear in mind his A-level courses in the timing of our eventual move from North Wingfield; I can see that for some clergy and their families it can be very difficult if moves have to be made at awkward times from the point of view of education. Sarah entered the teaching profession, her first post being at Grimsby, not too far away from us.

Michael took a travel agency course after graduating from Leicester University; and for most of the second half of the 1990s he was working abroad as a tour firm representative. Priscilla visited him in Turkey and Cyprus (revisiting her old haunts from her teaching days in the 1960s). She could hardly recognise Limassol where she had lived, as it had grown and developed into such an enormous tourist resort in the mean time. I later stayed at an hotel on the island of Gran Canaria when Michael was working there in the winter season. It was just perfect there in January – but not so nice getting back to England in a cold snap! Sarah moved to a school near Blackburn later in our time at North Wingfield; and there she became engaged to be married to Mr Norman Marshall, also in the teaching profession. Their wedding was on an extremely hot day in August, 1997, at St. Lawrence's Church, North Wingfield, a month before we left the parish. It made a nice climax to our time.

Several clergy whom I knew recommended that I should seek a "house-for-duty" appointment on leaving North Wingfield. At sixty-two, I could hardly expect to be offered another parish; but I could officially retire and receive a Church of England pension, while giving assistance in a parish or group of parishes where a rent-free house was offered, and expenses, but no other payment. It so happened that The Revd Jeff Chard, Rector of the Ironstone Benefice in North Oxfordshire, was looking for a priest to occupy the vicarage in one of the eight villages that his benefice served, and to share with him in the work. We were put in contact with each other; and so began a very pleasant chapter of my ministerial career. I will go on to describe it; but before I do so I will just add a few further reflections arising out of my time at North Wingfield.

Bishop Peter Dawes retired as Bishop of Derby in 1995, and in his place came Bishop Jonathan Bailey. Both bishops were equally friendly, and interested in the progress of our set-up. There were no larger team ministries in the diocese. Bishop Henry Richmond was suffragan Bishop of Repton all the time I was in Derbyshire; he had had a lot to do with the initial setting-up of the team ministry before I came; and he always was most supportive. During my years in the parish there were two Archdeacons of Chesterfield: Gerald Phizackerley for the greater part of my time, and later David Garnett. Both, I felt, were extremely good at their job, very caring, and somehow approached it all with a fairly light touch.

Though the Derby diocese was quite extensive geographically, stretching to the outskirts of Greater Manchester and Sheffield, there seemed to be a strong "family feeling" in the diocese; that was helped, I am sure, by having the annual clergy residential conference at Swanwick Conference Centre, right in the middle of the diocese. Through that it was possible to get to know a far wider range of diocesan clergy than those in one's own deanery or locality. The "hierarchy" of the diocese were also easily approachable there.

In our combined parish there were a number of Licensed Readers, who made a very big contribution to both the worshipping life of the churches and other aspects of the work entrusted to us. Two of the Readers were based primarily at St. Lawrence's, North Wingfield, though all officiated sometimes in churches other than their own. We had two centenaries to celebrate at St. Lawrence's while we were there. In 1992 the church organ was 100-years old. We had a concert, at which the organist of Derby Cathedral played the organ; and a special service with the Cathedral choir. The next year it was the turn of the church clock to reach its hundredth birthday. Its birthday present was electrification of the winding mechanism – a great relief for those who had hitherto voluntarily climbed up the tower to wind it by hand.

Money-raising efforts for that purpose included a sponsored walk by parishioners. It proved good that I was not free to take part in that, because I subsequently undertook my own sponsored walk, from the Blue Bell Inn, North Wingfield, to the Blue Bell Inn, South Wingfield, and back by a different route, some sixteen miles in all; I displayed photographs I had taken on the way; and the financial income was far more than I could have raised simply as part of a "community" walk, which wasn't nearly so far. I did one year walk the nine miles from North Wingfield to the Swanwick Conference, not as a sponsored effort, but for pleasure, fresh air and exercise on a lovely autumn day. Several people afterwards very kindly "sponsored" me – without any request from myself – towards money we were raising for, I think, the Church Urban Fund. The clock centenary was accompanied by a Victorian Weekend, which included a very good Victorian-style entertainment, put on by church and community members, and Songs of Praise accompanied by the local Salvation Army Band. People were invited to wear Victorian costume during the weekend. I let my "side-burns" grow, to look more the part in clerical morning dress with a black top hat.

Mention of the Salvation Army prompts me to say that we tried hard to maintain friendly relationships with

Keep Me Travelling

churches of other denominations in the area served by our united parish. North Wingfield had a small Methodist church, situated a bit of a way from St. Lawrence's and a Pentecostal church at the edge of one of the housing estates. Both of those, I felt, had a certain ministry to the people in the areas surrounding them; and we did undertake some public witness together, as well as supporting each other's special events. Clay Cross had churches of several denominations, which were brought together by an organisation known as "Christians in Clay Cross". That facilitated a good deal of cooperation. Alpha courses were introduced in parts of our parish in the latter part of my time there; they proved very helpful to "inquirers", who wanted to learn a bit more about the Christian Faith in a friendly and "unthreatening" setting. We owed a lot to the team vicar at Pilsley for introducing and facilitating that venture.

Priscilla and I left North Wingfield with mixed feelings. We were sorry to say "goodbye" to so many people whom we had got to know and like; but, as already explained, the expiry of my licence did seem the right time to make a move. Not surprisingly, perhaps, my successor as Team Rector was more in the evangelical community of the Church of England; that was the stance that was in the ascendant. Maybe the changes we made at North Wingfield church in the year or two before I left did serve to pave the way a bit for the more modern approach to worship that certainly took over after my time.

CHAPTER 10

Park-and-Ride; Virgin, Chiltern and Thames Trains; Foreign Underground Systems; "Once a Week" Bus Services.

After our rather eventful journey from Derbyshire, we moved into Horley Vicarage in September 1997. The eight villages that made up the Ironstone Benefice were all situated between two and six miles from Banbury, in a north-westerly direction from the town, and close to the Oxfordshire/Warwickshire border. So we were in a corner of the far-flung Oxford diocese; Windsor Castle was in the same diocese as us, and so was Milton Keynes – but within ten minutes' walk of our new home we could be in Coventry diocese. All the villages were small, none with a population of more than about four hundred, and several of them a good deal smaller than that. Yet they all had magnificent medieval churches, some of them Grade One listed. In each church worship was regularly offered on Sundays; some weekday services were held as well.

A very faithful band of parishioners did much to care for and beautify the parish church in each village. The churchwardens had considerable responsibilities – the Rector could only be resident in one of the villages. The very beautiful stretch of countryside in which the Ironstone villages were situated was not really on the "tourist trail", lying as it did east of the Cotswolds; but the scenery was really magnificent, and had an air of peace and tranquillity. None of the villages had a shop, though pubs were to be found – one or two of them notable for their excellent food as well as drink. People travelled to Banbury for shopping, or to the out-of-town supermarkets, which had a thriving trade. I would say that the area north of Banbury tended to look chiefly towards Birmingham and the Midlands for its main regional centres, while the villages south of Banbury looked more towards Oxford and London. So Banbury was something of a boundary town, situated in Oxfordshire, but very close to Northamptonshire and Warwickshire.

I was told that a hundred villages looked to Banbury as their main local centre – and that, being a bit of a way from any official county town, the country within a radius of about ten miles from Banbury had the unofficial title of "Banburyshire". Banbury itself had grown a good deal as light industry had expanded, and commuting had become very common. However, it still had the character of a market town, with some attractive old buildings; and about the turn of the millennium there opened a brand new shopping centre, called "Castle Quay", very close to the Oxford Canal, a busy waterway used for mainly leisure purposes. Big efforts have been made to encourage people from all parts of "Banburyshire" and beyond to use Banbury's facilities for their shopping trips, rather than to travel to other towns.

The name "Ironstone" given to our benefice denotes the very attractive yellowy stone, quarried locally, of which most of the older and newer buildings are constructed. It gives a very definite character to the villages. The villages in the care of The Revd Jeff Chard were, and are, as follows:

1. Wroxton, where the Rector lives. A "picture postcard" village, with its old cottages and village pond, as well as its fine church of All Saints, and "Wroxton Abbey", a fine Jacobean house on the site of the old Augustinian abbey, with extensive and beautiful grounds freely open to the public. Those who come from the USA to study there certainly are able to enjoy a most delightful corner of England. Wroxton church contains some monuments commemorating Lord North (a former prime minister) and members of his family. Wroxton Abbey was where he lived in the eighteenth century.

2. Horley, where Priscilla and I occupied the modern vicarage. Horley too has a very fine parish church, dedicated to St. Etheldreda, foundress of Ely Cathedral. A striking feature of the church is the very large medieval wall-painting of St. Christopher. A survey has recently been done of this and of the remains of other ancient wall-paintings in Horley church, with a view to some restoration being undertaken. Like all the Ironstone villages, Horley has become very much a commuter village. At the

end of the Second World War a large proportion of the people were engaged in agriculture. The character of the village has of course changed as that has become less and less the case. Horley has a thriving community life. A recently formed dramatic society put on an excellent village pantomime in February 2003.

3. Hornton. Further out from Banbury, and maybe partly for that reason, Hornton people have made enormous efforts to form a real village community. The local newspaper always seems to have more village news in the Hornton column than in that of any other local village. Ecclesiastically, Hornton has led the way in cooperation and fellowship between the Anglican and Methodist churches. A covenant has been formed, and the two churches share their life and worship to a very great extent. St. John the Baptist's Church, Hornton, also has some intriguing wall-paintings, including the "harrowing of hell", and the Black Prince dressed as St. George. Hornton has been described as the "quintessential English village". Nestling as it does in a hollow, surrounded by higher ground, and with a steep escarpment rising from one side of the village, it is full of character, with some fine old houses and a village green.

4. Shenington. Another lovely village, with a delightful church. Its Church of England Primary School is famous for its outstandingly high standards; and

places there are strongly sought after. Perhaps one would say that the village is predominantly the abode of fairly prosperous people. Average attendance at the parish church of the Holy Trinity is on the whole higher than in most of the other Ironstone villages.

5. Alkerton. Separated from Shenington by a dip, Alkerton is the sweetest place imaginable. It is very hilly, and the superb church of St. Michael and All Angels is built on a steep slope, the chancel and sanctuary being a bit of a climb to reach from the nave. It is barely half a mile from Shenington church. The two are run very closely together, with one Parochial Church Council for them both. Alkerton has two regular Sunday morning services a month, and is used for some weekday services, such as a monthly requiem and a quiet time of prayer.

6. Balscote. A small village between Wroxton and Shenington, set in most beautiful country. The community takes great pride in the Church of St. Mary Magdalene, a real showpiece. Balscote Methodist church works very closely with the Anglican church.

7. Drayton. The closest village to Banbury, but if you go down to where the church of St. Peter is situated, in a hollow below the village, Banbury might be a thousand miles away. The church is in a really beautiful rural setting. The village itself is so

definitely a village, and quite separate from the town. It has its own distinctive life.

8. Hanwell. A bit separate from the other villages of the Ironstone Benefice, and the only one situated to the east of the old Warwick road. The superb church is reputed to be where Cromwell's horses were stabled before the Civil War battle of Cropredy Bridge nearby. Again great thanks are due to a number of villagers who have done much to preserve and beautify the splendid church of St. Peter. It is a very wide church, and quite unlike any of the others in the benefice. Church people seem to be the leading lights of village life.

Seven of the eight churches have a service every Sunday (except for Benefice Service Sundays about eight times a year); Alkerton, as I mentioned has a service on two Sundays each month. So the Rector and his ministerial team have quite a bit of travelling around to do. Every church is the venue once a year for a Benefice Service; and on those Sundays that is the only service in the group of villages. So every effort is made to encourage people to come and meet the people of the other churches on those occasions. A certain of amount of opportunity for joining in social activities, and in study and discussion groups, is provided at benefice level. A benefice choir has been formed, and this choir leads the music at benefice services and on some other local church occasions.

The separate Parochial Church Councils, which make decisions for church life, building maintenance, finance, etc. in their own villages is supplemented by a Benefice Council, consisting of all the churchwardens and others who have benefice-wide responsibilities. I think the Revd Jeff Chard has done extremely well as Rector. When he came in 1996, he took over what had previously been two separate groups of churches. I was appointed to live in Horley Vicarage, with a licence lasting for five years. After the next bit, about transport, I will explain what happened when my licence expired.

From the railway point of view, Banbury is very well connected. Chiltern Railways provide two or three trains an hour to London (Marylebone), extended northwards beyond Banbury to Birmingham Snow Hill every half-hour, and to Stratford-upon-Avon every two hours; in fact a few Chiltern trains go beyond Birmingham, serving other places in the West Midlands. Diesel multiple-unit trains are used, the newer ones being called "Clubman" trains, with enhanced comfort. Great Western Link trains also go to Banbury from London (Paddington), but not so frequently, at intervals of about one and a half or two hours. Banbury has the good fortune to be on the Virgin Cross Country Trains network; and with the delivery of their new-style "Voyager" trains, their services have been increased. Bournemouth is reached from Banbury most hours; Reading, via Oxford, generally twice an hour; northbound trains run to Birmingham New Street, where a wealth of connections can be made, and nearly all the trains serving Banbury go on further north, to

Manchester, or to Edinburgh, Glasgow and even Aberdeen, either via Preston or Newcastle. Priscilla and I recently travelled by train from Dunbar (between Edinburgh and Newcastle) to Banbury, with changes en route at Newcastle and Birmingham, and the journey from Dunbar station to Banbury station took no more than six hours. Quite a lot of people commute daily from Banbury to London by train; and the fastest trains now take little more than an hour on that route.

For journeys to Heathrow Airport from Banbury it is convenient to use the regular National Express coach service, which starts from Wolverhampton. The coaches also go through to Gatwick (which may be able to be reached a bit more quickly by train); however, the Banbury to Heathrow coach journey is much quicker than by any other means of public transport, taking only about an hour and twenty minutes. Local buses in the Banbury area are largely provided by Stagecoach, who took over the southern division of Midland Red. Banbury had for many years been a Midland Red bus centre, a bit out on a limb from most of that former huge company's operations.

By the time we came to live in the district, rural bus services had been pretty drastically cut. The point is that people would not be likely to choose to live in the villages around Banbury if they did not have their own private transport. Brackley, a small and very attractive town east of Banbury, in Northamptonshire, still seems to justify a half-hourly bus service to and from Banbury, via the extensive residential area of Middleton Cheney. There is also a Stagecoach bus route linking Banbury with Oxford every one and a half hours. For through journeys it makes more sense to go by train, which is much quicker and more frequent; however, that long bus route serves a lot of intermediate communities, giving them a link with both Oxford and Banbury. "The Great Central Connexion" is an hourly bus service provided by Amos of Eydon, joining Banbury with Rugby, via the large residential area of Woodford Halse and Hinton, set in the Northamptonshire countryside, as well as the town of Daventry (not reachable by rail).

Stagecoach has a network of town buses in Banbury. There is talk about some possible improvements to local bus services, in the hope (I think) that motorists going into the town will be successfully tempted to leave their cars at home, and avoid some of the hassle of driving. Whether better bus services would have that effect is questionable, I must say – but in Oxford the local buses are very well used by all sections of the community, largely because parking of cars is so restricted and expensive. Oxford has a well-developed system of "park-and-ride", with large car parks at several sites on the edge of the city, from which frequent buses take motorists to the city centre.

We generally use that facility if we drive to Oxford. In Banbury there are quite good local bus services to those parts of the town where there are substantial numbers of non-car owners, but the diffuse nature of much of the newer development seems to be based on the assumption that pretty well everyone living there will use personal transport. The Ironstone villages have a few buses, but not many. Those that are on the slow and roundabout service between Banbury and Stratford-upon-Avon, which is run by the Warwickshire firm of Johnsons, do get several buses a day passing through them. Horley has a one-journey-a-week market day bus on Thursdays, run by Cheney Travel (a local firm); the bus serves Hornton as well. The Cherwell Villager system of operating specially adapted mini-buses suitable for some disabled people to use includes Horley on its Tuesday run, picking up at a number of villages; other groups of villages are served on other days.

They all have their regular passengers; the one time I used it, I was a bit afraid that I was taking up the seat of someone for whom it was a necessary lifeline. Living in Horley, I invested in an excellent Peugeot 100 cc scooter, rather a far cry from the earlier machines I had; it has automatic transmission (no clutch or gearchange), and is in some ways easier to ride than an ordinary bicycle. Its electric starter makes it all the more of a cinch. Having that bike means that Priscilla and I don't have awkward clashes when we both need or want to go to different places at the same time. We currently own a Citroën Xsara, obtained new in 1999 at a greatly discounted price in part-exchange for our previous car, from Autosave, who supply cars to clergy and people who work in certain fields where personal transport is needed for some kind of "caring" ministry.

The chapter heading mentions foreign underground systems. I seem to have tasted several in the last few years and been impressed by them. The Paris Metro is well known; the Marseilles one less so – it is quite new, and certainly whisked us around very efficiently. In 1998 I visited Berlin with Michael, our son in the travel trade. I was enormously struck by the excellent service provided by the U-Bahn (mainly underground), as well as the S-Bahn, surface level local railways. The unification of Berlin has brought a coming together of the two former transport systems – but the old East Berlin underground trains were very noticeably of a more basic and "utility"construction than the better appointed West Berlin ones. Priscilla, Peter and I visited Barcelona later that same year – and what a superb underground system we found there, as well as numerous bus services.

My most recent discovery of a Metro is that of Prague, where Michael and I spent a few days in March 2002. There are very good and frequent trains, but the stations have exits and entrances a good distance from where the stations actually are. You walk a bit of distance underground, so it is important to use the correct station exit for where you want to get to.

I was terribly puzzled one day; we had joined the Metro at a station entrance about five minutes' walk in the direction of the city centre from our hotel. When we got out at the same station on our return journey, I just couldn't think where we were on emerging from the station. We were very close to the river, in quite the opposite direction from our hotel. I came to see that the station was just about under the hotel, but access to it could be gained only by walking some way in a choice of two quite different directions! Again, as at Berlin, the trains that dated from Communist days were strikingly inferior to the more modern ones, and much plainer in design. The underground stations also had rather a look of austerity, and it took a bit of time to get used to the speed of the escalators. You really had to take care on joining and leaving them! I have also been with Michael to Brussels, and taken advantage of the excellent underground train service there.

Reference to our son Michael leads me to mention his marriage to Caroline Everard at Chiswick Parish Church, London, in 2002. The partly medieval church is just beside the Thames, in a remarkably peaceful and quiet location, away from the noise of traffic, although very close to the Hogarth roundabout on the A4. Michael and Caroline have sons called Luke and Harry; and Sarah and Norman, still living in Lancashire, have two boys a little older than them, named Joseph and Christopher. When we are with our grandchildren, Priscilla and I feel young again! Peter, our younger son, took a degree in English at Sussex University, and then a journalism course. He is currently employed by the *Leamington Courier* local weekly newspaper, as a reporter, and is being given considerable responsibility by the editor. It is nice for us that Peter is living and working not far away from Banbury, because it means that we can often see him.

My ministry in the Ironstone Benefice was of course very different from that which I had had as vicar or rector of parishes. The buck no longer stopped with me! What a feeling of relief! Also, not receiving a stipend, I was not under the same obligation to devote so much time to the affairs of the churches and the parishes. It was of course important that I should get to know the people of all the villages, and take as full a part as possible in the life of the communities that made up the benefice. I regularly led worship in all the churches. The Rector also had help from some other retired and non-stipendiary clergy living in the Banbury area.

When I went there first, Mrs Pamela Smith was training for ordained ministry; and the whole benefice was extremely pleased when she was, first, ordained deacon, and then a year later, priest, to serve in the Ironstone benefice, as well as to be chaplain of St. Katharine's Hospice, just outside Banbury. Pam was not "stipendiary", and she lived for some time in a house in Banbury, before moving into Horley Vicarage when the time came for us to vacate it. The parishes also had the benefit of two "Licensed Lay Ministers", to give Readers their official title nowadays. One, Mr John Straw, had exercised that ministry for many years. The other, Mrs Lindy Bridgeman, was licensed during my time, and was very well received indeed, and deservedly so.

I am so pleased to be able to say that when we did leave Horley, we didn't really leave at all. Priscilla and I purchased a modern house in Banbury within walking distance from the town centre. The house has a small but very pleasant garden. Jeff Chard very generously invited me to continue as a member of the ministerial team of the Ironstone Benefice. Of course we missed many of the features of actually living in one of the villages –

including the daily morning newspaper delivery round that both Priscilla and I had been doing for several years in Horley; that had helped to keep us fit, as we always did it on foot, and it had kept us in close touch with villagers.

Actually we are both now delivering free newspapers every week in the roads around where we live. At present, I am ministering in the Ironstone churches about two or three Sundays a month, and sometimes helping in other churches in the locality. I am keeping on the secretaryship of Horley Parochial Church Council; and have now that of Drayton PCC as well. Priscilla and I try to support a range of activities and events in the Ironstone Benefice. We have not had to say "goodbye" to our friends. When not involved elsewhere we like to worship in the parish church of where we live, namely St. Leonard's, Grimsbury, where we find much friendliness. Moving such a short way (four and a half miles, to be exact) means that we can keep up all that we were previously involved in locally.

For Priscilla that includes the Banbury and District Art Society; she is well involved in that, and her paintings are included in their exhibitions. She has also been doing some home tutoring of boys and girls who have been unable to attend school for one reason or another. I am keeping on with the Monday afternoon bridge club at St. Hugh's Church, Banbury, for the running of which I have been responsible for a few years.

In the summer months I like to go to play croquet at our nearest club, at Kenilworth, Warwickshire. It is a very good club, with a croquet section in a predominantly tennis and squash club. Croquet competitions and tournaments are held, as well as matches against other clubs. One day in 2003 I played for the first time on the Oxford University croquet lawns in the University Parks, a superb setting; Kenilworth had a match against the university. It is good that a fair number of undergraduates have taken up the game, and pass their enthusiasm on to others who come up to Oxford University. Priscilla and I still sometimes go riding, from very friendly stables not far away, for a hack in beautiful countryside, and Priscilla helps elsewhere with Riding for the Disabled.

The proximity of the Oxford Canal to where we live makes it easy to go for pleasant walks on the towpath; and of course we have the magnificent "Banburyshire" country easily accessible by car to enjoy on foot. Banbury is really an excellent centre. It is a long way from the sea, I know – but, being so centrally placed in England, we have been able to do day trips to visit relations and friends, and attend special events, as far afield as Norfolk, Cambridgeshire, Essex, Kent, Sussex, London, Surrey, Hampshire, Dorset, Bristol, and Derbyshire. It is possible to do a day trip by car to our daughter's home near Blackburn; when she and her family visited us for a day, they were able to have six and a half hours with us, without an excessively early start or late return.

CHAPTER 11

"Keep me Travelling ..."

This chapter is devoted to developments in transport that have occurred during my lifetime so far, and their implications for society and for the lives of individuals. A very big generalisation would be to say that in Britain and the more developed countries of the world, private transport has very largely taken over from public transport for the majority of journeys that most people make. When I was a boy, in wartime conditions, the use of cars was extremely restricted; many of those who owned cars laid them up for the duration of the war. When private motoring came back – and it wasn't really until the end of petrol rationing in 1950 that cars were regularly used by their owners for any substantial amounts of travel – cars were still owned only by a minority of families, who were more prosperous than the average family. Motorcycles were used a fair amount, particularly by men travelling to or from their work. For short journeys bicycles were a common form of transport – and people thought little of walking a mile or two.

Travelling by bus, which, as I mentioned earlier, was still cheap in the early 1950s, was an absolutely normal part of life for most men and women, boys and girls; and in cities and larger towns very comprehensive and frequent bus services made local travel quite easy. Some larger cities still had trams plying on their main streets for fifteen years or so after the Second World War. Some changed over from trams to trolleybuses, a form of transport lasting into the 1960s. Other places, such as Bristol, which I remember so well from my younger days, made it their policy to standardise on diesel-engined buses when they abandoned their trams; petrol-engined buses had just about all been replaced by diesels by the end of the 1940s, except for some single-deckers operating in country districts. If city and town dwellers had frequent bus services at hand to meet most of their local travel needs, those living in villages and rural areas in the years following the Second World War often had reasonable services as well, though it was necessary for them to consult or to know the timetable.

Larger towns would have quite a network of out-of-town bus routes radiating from them, providing links with other towns within twenty miles or so, as well as the surrounding villages. Hourly frequencies were common on inter-urban bus routes which called at intermediate villages, and the same frequency was maintained until quite late in the evening. On Sundays both urban and rural bus services were a bit reduced (particularly in the morning), but from midday onwards many routes operated much the same on Sundays as on weekdays. Different companies had rather different policies regarding provision of Sunday buses. In some places they did not start until the afternoon, but as the 1950s progressed, and services generally became reduced, a latent demand for Sunday morning buses began to be rather better met. In fact, even as late as the 1980s, when we went to live at Swindon, I found that Sunday bus services were non-existent before about 2 p.m; however, in spite of afternoon frequencies being gradually whittled down to become only once an hour on most routes, the hourly service did begin running much earlier in the day, from about 9 a.m.

It was as cars increased in number on the roads that bus operators ran into economic difficulties; and it became more difficult for non-car owners to get about in the evenings and on Sunday afternoons. The operators' response to getting fewer passengers was very often to provide fewer buses, so that it became a vicious circle, and the services were even less attractive to potential passengers. I am not a transport economist, and can only look on what I saw from outside the industry. However, I do feel that some "economy" measures that were taken by bus operators in the third quarter of the twentieth century were short-sighted, and gave the impression that the bus services were being provided only for the benefit of a "captive market", who had no other means of travelling.

Little seemed to be done to try to attract people to use the buses, until in the fourth quarter of the century there seemed to develop a much stronger effort to discern the "potential" of particular bus services and take appropriate action accordingly. I suppose it was mainly after the "deregulation" of bus services in the 1980s that a fresh look was taken at how often buses ought to run on particular routes to realise the potential of those routes. People had been put off by long intervals between buses;

they were far more likely to use them if they could travel at the times when they needed or wanted to travel – and for local journeys that was an even more important consideration than for longer journeys. Buses in recent years have also on the whole been made more pleasant to travel on, with more comfortable seats and better leg-room; also on many buses there is easier access, with lower floors and less steep steps.

Those enormous numbers of double and single-decked buses manufactured by Bristol Commercial Vehicles, and with very attractively styled bodies by Eastern Coach Works that were to be seen in many parts of the country during the 1950s, 60s and 70s were mechanically very sound, and gave their operators excellent service; but I sometimes wondered whether the comfort of passengers was given quite sufficient consideration. People were subjected to rather a lot of vibration. Seats were just too close to the seats in front to give taller passengers sufficient leg-room. The substitution of plastic ("leather-look") seats for the more attractive and more comfortable moquette ones was a backward step as far as passengers were concerned. Right into the 1960s it was quite common for buses to be running around with no provision for interior heating in winter.

Many companies gave prospective passengers less and less in the way of route information displayed on the buses – just a final destination and route number took the place of the former more comprehensive displays. Rear and side destination indicators completely disappeared (with a few exceptions, such as London). The gradual removal of the conductor slowed journeys down, as drivers had to take the fares from a queue of waiting passengers at stops; and the kind of help that friendly conductors were able to offer to elderly or disabled passengers was no longer available. Though smoking had generally been banned in the lower saloon of double-deckers, people travelling on single-deckers could not get away from tobacco smoke. The notice that some operators put up, "Smokers are requested to occupy rear seats" was not enforceable, and was frequently ignored. Of course bus operators were concerned as to how economies could be made; but when they were at the expense of the passengers' comfort or convenience, they may have actually proved to be rather false economies.

It is understandable that bus companies should wish to carry as many passengers as possible on any one journey, and should do that by serving as many stops as they can along the corridors on which they run. There is a subtle balance between the provision of frequent stops, and the wish of passengers to get to their destination without undue delay. My impressions in mid-century were that buses tended to be too slow on the whole; and that was particularly the case with many inter-urban journeys, which kept on leaving main roads to serve villages which were down country lanes.

The Eastern Counties company, I think, must have held the record for slow bus journeys. I suppose it was good that people living in tucked-away villages had as much public transport as they did; but it made journeys extremely tedious for people travelling between two towns that were twenty miles apart as the crow flies, if the buses linking them added enormously to the direct mileage, and kept on travelling at a very leisurely pace through hamlets and housing estates that required substantial diversions.

As people got more used to travelling by car, they became less tolerant of the slowness of so many bus services. So there has been quite a speeding up on many longer routes in more recent years. In the early 1990s there was published quite a thick volume entitled *Great Britain Bus Timetable*, and updated editions appeared for several years. Unfortunately it is no longer produced, as presumably there was insufficient demand for it. A 1996 edition in my possession shows how well served many parts of the country were then, though I know there have been a good many reductions in more recent years.

The timetable book does not show local routes in towns, on which I suppose the majority of passenger miles by bus are travelled. It interests and in some ways surprises me that while most people I know would never dream of using an ordinary service bus for any journey (except perhaps on a visit to London) there are still enough passengers to keep inter-urban bus services going. My impression is that most people who travel on them do so for fairly short journeys, between their home and their main local centre; and the longer routes provide facilities for an enormous range of different passenger journeys that overlap one another. I referred in an earlier chapter to the "deregulation" of local bus services which occurred in the 1980s.

Traditionally, when large companies operated buses over a widespread area, they were able to provide a comprehensive network through use of the profits made on many journeys; they would help to subsidise the routes and journeys that were less well patronised. By about the early 1970s, when the National Bus Company had come into existence, some of its more rural components threatened to withdraw services that were making a loss. Legislation came in by which local authorities could subsidise bus services that were thought to be "socially necessary". The Thatcher government thought that much of the money spent on such subsidies was being wastefully used. So to make the whole operation of bus services more economic, major changes were introduced. Services were put into two categories, "Registered" and "Tendered". Registered services were (and are) those which operators run as a commercial venture, with no subsidy. The former monopoly rights of established operators in clearly defined areas were abolished.

Competition was encouraged, though quality controls were tightened. Main urban and inter-urban services were generally registered by their existing operators. In few places did competition really take off. Services that were not thought to be commercially viable were put out to tender by local authorities to be run as subsidised operations (if they were thought to be worth continuing at all); and those authorities allocated their subsidies to operators who submitted the lowest tenders, generally. That is still how it is now; and tendered services tend to be the more rural ones, linking towns with villages. Also many routes which are registered for weekday daytimes are put out to tender for evenings and Sundays; the result may be that a different firm runs them at those times. In Banbury there is one local route where Stagecoach until recently ran the evening service commercially on Fridays and Saturdays; but on other evenings, and all day on Sundays, the service was provided by Cheney Travel as a tendered and subsidised operation.

The long distance coach services which I remember from the 1950s providing a much slower but cheaper alternative to railway travel over much of the country, and often serving places that were not on the rail network, became unified in the form of National Express, when the National Bus Company came into existence. The opportunity was taken to make it into a truly national system, with carefully planned connections at a number of major points, so that people could travel by coach, if not quite "from anywhere to anywhere", at any rate not far off the claims of that slogan that was used.

National Express white coaches became a familiar sight on the main roads of Britain; and their use of motorways speeded up their journeys. When "deregulation" came in, National Express had the resources to see off most of the competition that the Conservative government encouraged; and when the National Bus Company was dissolved, National Express continued as a privatised company, with its coaches in the same white livery. During the 1990s and 2000s, it seems that National Express has reduced its operations somewhat. That may be partly on account of the privatised railways taking a commercial approach; there is on the whole now a smaller differential between coach fares and the off-peak, Saver and Apex fares of the railway companies. Also, although railway punctuality certainly cannot be relied on, the increases of traffic on the roads of course affect coaches as well as cars; and congestion can play havoc with long distance coach timetables.

While the conditions that encourage car owners to switch to buses or coaches are very limited indeed (mainly "park-and-ride" provision and difficult car parking in cities and towns that are trying to reduce traffic congestion), the railways are very certainly and successfully trying to provide a service that motorists will use in preference to their own cars for a large number of journeys. An obvious example is travel to and from central London. Car-owning commuters wouldn't think of driving to the capital. The roads and parking spaces couldn't accommodate their cars if they tried to do so.

A problem arises, however, when car parks at stations from which commuters travel get filled up quite early in the day. At Banbury an overflow car park has been opened for rail travellers, a good five minutes' walk from the station. People travelling to London or elsewhere by train after the morning peak now generally go straight to that overflow car park, knowing that they cannot expect to park any nearer. The "Parkway" stations that have been built near motorways and major roads outside towns have proved very useful in providing motorists with easy access to railway services.

There is a good deal of publicity encouraging people to use trains rather than their own cars for visits to large or historic cities (e.g. Birmingham and York), and places popular with tourists (e.g. Warwick Castle), and discounts at some attractions are offered if people show their rail tickets. At Warwick Castle and Chatsworth, among other places, special rail and entrance tickets are on sale at a reduced price (in the case of Chatsworth House, with coach travel from and to Chesterfield station included). I think too that many people who own cars choose to use the railways instead if they are making long journeys of 150 miles or more, and particularly if they can make use of offers of fares well below the standard rates.

During my lifetime I have seen very big changes in the railways of our land. The disappearance of steam trains in favour of diesel and electric traction is one important feature; and speeds have consequently increased quite dramatically. A real watershed came with the Beeching Report of 1963. Though some uneconomic services had been withdrawn before then, the plans that Dr Beeching unravelled were to close practically all stations that were rurally situated, unless they served substantial numbers of commuters.

In Victorian days, before there was motorised road traffic, lots of villages had wayside railway stations carrying their name; more often than not the station was a bit of distance from the village, but it provided much quicker transport than the carrier's cart, and offered access to a wide range of destinations. Some of these stations were on main lines, served by stopping trains, while expresses sped through them; others were on branch lines, which connected with the main lines. By the late 1960s a very large number of branch and secondary railway lines had ceased to exist (maintenance of their infrastructure was far too costly in relation to their meagre revenues from passengers); and closure of small stations on main lines enabled fast trains to be all the faster, without getting held up by slow ones.

First, it was bus services, which went into village centres, and then it was private transport, that took away the patronage of local rural railways. Dr Beeching saw the future of the railways in terms of what railways could do better than road transport – in particular the carrying of heavy loads of passengers into and out of London and other large cities for commuting, business and leisure travel; and really fast running over long distances (e.g. London to Edinburgh, Bournemouth to Manchester, York to Bristol, etc.), greatly exceeding the speed of any road transport.

It is noteworthy that the London Underground system is carrying more passengers than ever. Trunk journeys in Greater London take much longer on the congested roads. Some other cities are now introducing more rail-based local transport services, as in Newcastle and its environs, Greater Manchester, Sheffield, and the Birmingham/Black Country corridor. A new style of tram is coming into existence, running mainly on segregated track, but in some cases sharing city streets with other traffic. It will be interesting to see how this concept develops, and how far it eases road congestion, if car owners can be tempted to use these light-rail systems in preference to their own cars.

Air travel has expanded vastly in my lifetime. The problem is where new airports can be built to accommodate the increasing number of flights. Nevertheless, transport by air is in most cases only for journeys of considerable length. The time taken in getting to and from airports and going through the necessary procedures there means that the actual flight can be only quite a small proportion of the total journey time.

At Marlborough College we used to sing at the end of term fifty years ago, "Old Grandpapa he trundled home all in his chaise and pair. It's train today and motor car, and soon we'll go by air." That "soon" has taken a long time coming. I think people had visions of a day when an enormous number of quite short journeys would be made by vertical-take-off aircraft; it has become all the more difficult to envisage that now – and the thought of "air congestion" is even more distasteful than road congestion! Who knows how people will be travelling around Britain and around their local areas when the twenty-second century comes in?

I find it interesting to realise that the cars of today are not fundamentally different from the cars of my boyhood years. Of course there are lots of refinements now, not the least of them being the standard of interior heating and ventilation. The same principles of the internal combustion engine hold good. Sixty years ago, who ever would have thought that there would be such things as seat belts in cars? But then neither was it envisaged that journeys by road in Britain would be able to be done at anything like the average speeds of today. Before there were motorways, when dual carriageways were rare, when most roads were much narrower and many bends much sharper, and when there were not the useful lane markings that there are today, you did well to keep up an average speed of thirty miles an hour on a journey of any length.

A slow lorry in front could be impossible to overtake safely. Road accidents and casualties were much more numerous than they are now, even though there was only a fraction of today's number of cars on the roads. Driving tests had only come in during the 1930s; so there were lots of drivers who had had very little in the way of tuition, and who "did their own thing" when they were at the wheel of a car.

Furthermore, most cars of the first half of the twentieth century were a good deal less stable than today's cars are; you were that bit more likely to get into a skid or a situation that you couldn't control than you are nowadays with such greatly improved safety features built into car design. The proportion of motorcycles to cars was much higher when I was a boy – though that may not apply to London now! Actually, unlike the 1940s and 50s, when motorcycles were largely owned by men (not women) who couldn't afford cars, they are used very largely now by those who would find it difficult to purchase a second car, but whose transport needs cannot be fully met if there is only one car in the family.

As I mentioned earlier, the rather unladylike requirements for being able to ride powered two-wheelers, such as managing heavy kick-starters, have largely been eliminated; and both sexes are to be seen sporting modern-style scooters and larger bikes as well. Also big efforts have been made to improve safety. It is now compulsory to have off-road training and pass a basic test before riding any kind of motorcycle on a public road.

Ordinary bicycles have gone through some big design changes; and modern ones are multi-geared, enabling riders to travel at much faster average speeds without undue exertion. I have not used one since the early 1980s, when I felt it was safer to go on a powered bike which could keep up with the speed of the traffic. Many motorists tend to overtake cyclists with very little room to spare, and it can be quite nerve-racking.

Those local authorities which want to encourage cycling are now trying to make provision for segregating cyclists from motor traffic as much as possible. Whether, in view of that, bicycles will come back to being used by adults in much greater numbers remains to be seen. It sometimes surprises me that children have so much freedom to use bicycles on busy roads with only voluntary training and testing.

I haven't mentioned taxis in my review of transport developments in my lifetime. It is useful to know that they are generally available if one wishes to make a journey for which there is no suitable public transport – and if several people are travelling together, it can work out for some journeys hardly more expensive than paying separate fares on buses. Certainly taxis are in many places in considerable demand in the evenings and on Sundays, when bus services are so limited or non-existent; and they also have a useful and valued function in view of the strong message, "Don't drink and drive".

It is often said that people are more likely to keep healthy if they walk a good deal. It is all a matter of one's life-style, and how much walking can easily be built into it. It is tempting to take out one's car for short runs for the sake of saving five or ten minutes – but it may not be a very good habit to get into. Many people now seem quite surprised if they discover that someone has walked a mile or more to get to where they want to go; when I was young, it was quite commonplace to do so. Yet it is said that walking is a major British pastime, and a popular leisure activity, with its own appropriate kit. It is one thing to go on a country ramble or hike equipped with rucksack and boots. It is another to choose to walk from where you are to where you want to go, if you can allow sufficient time. To get into the way of doing that can prove really beneficial to one's general health, and can prove to be a very effective "feel-good factor".

CHAPTER 12

"... along with You."

In this final chapter the theme is the developments that I have perceived in attitudes to God and to religion over the years of my life, and the effects of those developments on the Christian Church in particular and on society in general. In very many respects I have travelled "from the old to the new" – and that is as true of the spiritual aspects of life as of any other. As I have sought to exercise the ministry to which I have believed that I have been called, I have tried to discern where God has been leading me and others. I think the shortcomings of that ministry have been the results of my getting out of step with God, and being too keen to go my own way and not His. The most rewarding times have been those when I have been most conscious of "travelling along with Him", and thus have been able to draw upon spiritual resources much greater than my own.

From what I have written it will be clear that I grew up in a strongly Christian environment, both at home and at school. I regard that as a great privilege, and have no idea how my life would have developed if that had not been the case. Yet the Christian background to my boyhood years was of its time, and very different, I am sure, in many respects from the kind of Christian background that today's youngsters can reasonably expect to have. In the 1930s and 40s there was still a sense permeating society in this country of Christian values being those that ought to be pursued. There was a greater overall respect for God and for Jesus Christ. Prayer was more natural to more people than is the case now. Churchgoing was more general. Those who seldom or never went were more likely to feel that nevertheless they did have a religion, and very large numbers of such people claimed to be "Church of England".

They recognised their parish church as being in a real sense theirs, and the local clergy as having some sort of responsibility towards them. Many would expect to be visited by a representative of their parish church, and if that did not happen they would feel that the church deserved rather a black mark. The clergy themselves had rather freer entry into people's homes than is generally the case today, were more likely to be consulted about things that mattered to people, and had many requests to officiate at the baptisms, marriages and funerals of their parishioners, regardless of the strength or weakness of their general links with the Church.

My coming to consider the possibility of applying for Ordination sprang from my observing and experiencing Christianity's power for good in people's lives, and from my strong admiration of certain clergy whom I came to know. That process certainly began in my childhood, though it was not until I was aged twenty-one that I developed sufficient of a sense of vocation to feel it was right to ask for that sense of vocation to be tested by the Church of England's official procedures. As mentioned earlier, I am sure that the time of my Confirmation and the preparation for it had a very formative influence. I personally am glad that I was not Confirmed before the age of fifteen, because I doubt whether I would have been quite so ready to take that step at an earlier age; it might not have meant so much to me.

My early life may appear to have been rather sheltered in some respects. That may seem a funny thing to say in view of the fact that I started boarding school at the age of six. However, my closest contacts with others, whether adults or my own contemporaries, were very much with those whose backgrounds were fairly similar to my own. It was not until I was called up into the Army at the age of eighteen that I found myself living side by side with young men who had come from very different backgrounds. Most of them had had little in the way of specific Christian nurture. What experience of the Church they had had was not on the whole very positive. They accepted the Church as "being there", with a certain ministry to those who wished to make use of the services it offered, but not as having very much to offer on a regular basis to strong and healthy young men.

I did find some in the Army who did have a valued link with their local church at home; in those days the churches did lay on a good deal of club-based activity for young people, and enabled the deepening of many friendships. Also Sunday Schools were often well-attended, though sometimes they could hardly cope with the numbers who came; where it was a case of children being "sent" by their non-churchgoing parents to Sunday Schools that had got into a bit of a rut, it is hardly surprising that children's enthusiasm was lacking; and when they left as soon as their parents would allow them to do so, they did not carry away with them a very high regard for the Church.

In retrospect, from this point in time, I can see that during the 1950s big efforts were being made by the churches to make up the ground lost by wartime conditions. There seems to have been a widespread vision of bringing back the vitality and the characteristics of the pre-war church – not so much of bringing in something new, fitted for the post-war world. People on the whole seemed quite content to go on using the old Prayer Book services and the traditional hymns. Those who wanted something new dropped out, regarding the church as stagnant. Excellent work was certainly done in many churches and parishes.

There were some clergy who were ahead of their time, and who had imaginative ideas for reaching people who had not got a background of regular church attendance. Yet while there were those who felt that the "old-fashioned" image of the church was an obstacle to church growth, many other regular attenders liked the church being old-fashioned, didn't want change, and found a certain comfort in continuing the rituals and singing the hymns that they had known from childhood. While such people remained, and continued to form a fairly big proportion of the members of congregations, there was little incentive in many churches to look for ways of moving on. It was thus possible for local churches to keep going (but that is not to say to fulfil their potential) on inherited faith and patterns of worship passed down through generations, on inherited demand for the "occasional offices" (baptisms, weddings, funerals), on inherited expectations of a plentiful supply of Confirmation candidates, and, dare I say, on inherited money – for parish churches in those days did not have to be anything like fully self-supporting financially; vicars and rectors received their stipends by means of historic endowments. Churches could "pay their way" without their members having to dig very deeply into their pockets.

Those churches that did have "Christian Stewardship" programmes discovered a potential of giving (not just of money, but also of time and talents) that had never previously been properly tapped. So differentials in the income of parishes became enormous, and unrelated to the size and affluence of the regular congregation. Some people resisted "Stewardship" largely on the grounds of their traditional "fund-raising" events, which they saw almost as the backbone of church life; but such attitudes were shown to be very faulty – a wet day for the fête could have disastrous financial effects. Also the tradition of giving the vicar or rector the "Easter Offering" was a cop-out from the responsibility of seeing that he was properly reimbursed for the expenses that he incurred in the course of his parochial ministry. The variations in size of Easter offerings bore no relation to the sums paid out by the clergy for travel and office expenses.

By the time that I came to be ordained, at the beginning of the 1960s, fifteen years had elapsed since the end of the Second World War – and the mood in society and Church was no longer so much one of recreating the better features of pre-war life, but of moving on into a future with new opportunities.

Certainly the worse features of pre-war life had largely been overcome; there was not the unemployment that had been such a scourge of the 1930s, and the post-war "welfare state" had removed a lot of the fear and insecurity that went with being among the poorer section of society. The "success", if that is the right word, of a good many churches in the 1950s, where numbers of worshippers increased, and morale rose, was in fact very largely in places where middle-class people formed a large proportion of the congregation, and in university cities in particular. I wrote earlier about my experiences of the religious dimension of life at Cambridge.

What I did not mention was the very great strength and influence of Great St. Mary's, the University Church, while Mervyn Stockwood (later Bishop of Southwark) was Vicar; huge crowds of undergraduates came to the 8.30 p.m. services there on Sundays, with opportunities afterwards to ask questions of the preacher; and series of sermons, largely by visiting preachers, covered so many different aspects of Christian belief and morals, and the various responsibilities of the Christian community corporately and of individual Christians in relation to the big social issues of the time. Side by side with the University Church was Holy Trinity Church, where the Evangelical constituency met for a late evening service, also at 8.30 p.m. on Sundays, seen as an opportunity to present the Gospel and encourage a personal response from interested inquirers and from any present who were deeply and emotionally moved by the message they had heard and the experience of Christian worship.

What happened during the 1960s was that the churches sought positive ways of countering the general fall-off in attendance at worship; and the two very different ways in which that problem was chiefly addressed still have their counterparts now in the two different styles of church life that exist side by side in the Church of England, and to some extent also within (not just between) other denominations. To sum up one of the responses to declining Christian belief and practice, I can just use the phrase "Honest to God". A book with that title was published in 1963; its author was The Right Revd John Robinson, Bishop of Woolwich, whom I mentioned in an earlier chapter as a most inspiring and stimulating lecturer in theology at Cambridge University. *Honest to God* crystallised a great deal of scholarly thinking, and challenged its readers to re-think what they really did believe Christianity was all about.

Those who shared John Robinson's standpoint were very anxious that people should not be prevented from finding a strong personal Christian faith by misunderstandings about what was rightly to be seen as symbolic language in the Scriptures. People were being put off from any serious consideration of Christianity by having the idea that figurative sayings were meant to be taken literally. At Christmas people were expected to sing

"He came down to earth from Heaven, who is God and Lord of all." What did that notion convey? Heaven as some place far away? Some movement in space, which led to a tiny baby appearing, via a virgin's womb, in a "manger" (not a word in most people's normal vocabulary), the one place where there was peace in an overcrowded small town in a part of the world where Christians have for long now been only a small minority of the resident population? And was Easter to be understood largely in terms of an empty tomb and a uniquely reanimated corpse? What became known as "South Bank Religion", very greatly inspired by the thinking of John Robinson, gained the name "radical", which literally meant "getting to the roots". What was the kernel of the nut? What was the bathwater and what was the baby?

It was seen as a very important part of the Christian evangelistic effort that the heart of Christianity should be identified with a quality of invincible love embodied in Jesus, and still to be embodied in his Church – love that is built into the on-going purpose of the very power behind all life and all existence. The three words of St. John, "God is Love", no Christians would dispute; "South Bank Religion" was convinced that they needed rather a different sort of "unpacking" from so much conventional Christian teaching which did not take sufficient account of scientific advances or of the ways that people think to-day. I found all that very stimulating in the 1960s, and still do.

The other approach to evangelism in the 1960s took a strong line of resistance to that kind of radicalism. Not only those who regarded themselves as in the "evangelical" camp, but also many churchmen of a more Anglo-Catholic stance, held notions of the authority of the Bible or of the Church that they felt to be under threat. The framework in which the Good News was presented in the Scriptures and in church tradition was regarded as itself integrally bound up with the Good News. The more evangelical people maintained that Christians have no right to question what the Bible says; this is the word of God, they insisted. Often Billy Graham would preface his strong affirmations by the words, "The Bible says". Behind that lay a different understanding of the make-up of the Bible and the origins of its constituent books from the general consensus of Biblical scholars.

Also those who set enormous store by inherited church traditions and teachings (which often had no biblical origin) claimed that the Catholic Church (including in their view the Church of England) had a divinely-given authority, focused in its ordained ministry. That authority carried with it the responsibility of passing on its inheritance of belief and structure and discipline to each new generation. Fresh thinking about doctrine and practice risked turning into an abuse of the Church's true authority. While, in the Church of England, Evangelicals and Anglo-Catholics generally went their own separate ways, differing not only in their emphasis, but in giving almost contradictory teaching about the sacraments and the disciplines required of Christians, yet they both saw the missionary task in terms of "guarding the deposit" – not making changes in the thought patterns that have underlain the life and teaching of the Christian community for centuries past.

My ministry, as I have already explained, has generally been in churches which have not identified themselves with a particular brand of churchmanship, rather "middle-of-the-road", trying to accommodate the most helpful insights from all ecclesiastical "parties". But the middle of the road can be a dangerous place; you have things coming at you from different directions at once. Churches with a very definitely high-church or low-church stance are unlikely to have in their congregations people from the opposite end of the spectrum. Such churches are most often found in towns, where parishioners can easily attend a nearby church of another parish which is more of their style.

In rural and semi-rural areas parish churches are more likely to try to accommodate worshippers of rather differing views of churchmanship, because the parish is a more clearcut identity than it usually is in towns, and parishioners like to feel that their local church is their church. It makes less sense to go to a church which serves a different community from the one in which they live. I have always found among the worshippers in the churches where I have served people who have come from different ecclesiastical backgrounds; and as I wrote earlier, I have regarded it as important to be sensitive to the various expectations of different worshippers; though

I have sometimes been criticised by Anglo-Catholics, Evangelicals, and Liberal church people for not seeming to support their stance as much as they would have liked.

What I fear has been happening in the last decade or so is a certain hardening of attitudes, where some Christians within the Church of England itself have seen things very differently from fellow-members. I have explained something of the impact of that upon church life in North Wingfield parish. I think this hardening has come about largely because of the growing confidence and influence of Evangelicals in the Anglican Church, as they have increased their proportion of the total number of churchgoers.

Some recent controversies, such as that over homosexuality, have split the Christian community down the middle, Evangelicals and liberals generally being on different sides, and Christian charity has often seemed to be sadly lacking. I believe that in the near future some very big efforts will be made to clarify where different groups of Christians stand in their interpretation of the Bible and in their view of the nature of its authority; it is a shame if members of the same branch of the Christian Church regard each other as being in error, and do not really try hard enough to understand each other's deeply held convictions. The real divisions in the Church now seem not so much to be between different denominations as to cut across denominational boundaries.

During my years of ministry I have noticed big changes in the worship regularly offered to God. I have already mentioned the changing forms of service, which have largely supplanted the *Book of Common Prayer*. The *Alternative Service Book* has come and gone. Common Worship has a much greater flexibility about it; and for that reason largely those leading worship according to the services which it contains need to make some very thorough preparation beforehand of the presentation and content of the whole service. Where it is done well and imaginatively, it can be most inspiring. I have noticed a much wider range of hymns coming into regular use, with many written in the last few decades becoming firm favourites, such as "Tell out, my soul, the greatness of the Lord", "We have a Gospel to proclaim", "The Servant King", "Bind us together, Lord" and many others. New hymn-books have been published to meet modern demand.

There has been more use of very informal chorus-type songs in worship, not just in children's services. The concept of "All Age" services has been worked on very thoroughly; I mentioned earlier how I thought The Revd Leonard Woodcock at Thundersley in the 1960s was ahead of his time in the kind of "family" worship that he devised, and which older as well as younger people loved, and what a lot I learned from him. Things have moved on a lot since then, and informality has become much more the order of the day; how important it is that the kind of informality that develops does not take away from the dignity that is proper to the worship of God. There is a real art in getting that right.

The above principle applies also to baptisms, weddings and funerals, which I believe are generally conducted in a much more imaginative way than used often to be the case. More efforts are made to "personalise" these services, and that is helped by the Common Worship liturgies, with their flexibility. In the days when large town parishes had more of these "occasional offices" than they could really cope with, it is perhaps not surprising that some clergy got into the way of taking them in a rather perfunctory manner, particularly if the families concerned had no previous links with the church. But now I do think these services often make much more impact on those present; and pastoral contacts associated with them are regarded as important. Far fewer people now ask for the baptism of their children, because the spiritual significance of the event is not at all clear to them – but they still can have the party that has traditionally gone with the baptism; I have even known that to be called a "christening", without there being any religious ceremony at all.

As regards weddings, the Church is now "in the market", because civil marriage ceremonies have become so attractive an alternative to many couples; no longer do they have to be in register offices, but all sorts of pleasant venues are now available. The reception then follows on at the same place, without the delay and inconvenience of travelling. So we may well understand if those who would previously have chosen a church wedding for the attractive ambience are now choosing civil marriage in a hotel or stately home instead. It is those who really value the spiritual significance of the service, and the opportunity of dedicating their married life to God, who are more likely now to request to be married in church. The churches may be able to serve them better if they have fewer weddings to conduct. Funerals have rather changed their emphasis in more recent years. People now want an occasion more centred on the earthly life of the one who has died, with thanksgivings and remembrances, rather than a service which focuses more on life beyond death.

Certainly funerals today require very careful preparation, and the bereaved family often wishes to share in that preparation. Fewer funerals take place in parish churches (though that is more true of towns than villages); and again many feel that having a cremation service all under the same roof of the crematorium saves the splitting of it into two parts, with what may be quite a long journey in between them, if the local church is used for the first part. The widespread use of cars now means that many funerals are much better attended; and it is quite common for all who have come to be invited to a gathering with refreshments afterwards.

Where a church has a churchyard which is still open for burials, it will probably find that a large proportion of those who die in the parish will have a service in the church, followed by burial in the churchyard. But space in churchyards is getting less and less, and many can take no more new graves. I have noticed growing development of "ashes plots" in churchyards, enabling families to have a "sacred space" in which to focus their remembrance of loved ones who have been cremated; and often their names are inscribed in a *Book of Remembrance*.

While there are certainly many imaginative efforts to help people to find and develop their own personal Christian faith (including informal courses such as Alpha and Emmaus), such success as these efforts may have is hardly scratching the surface of England's present-day society and culture. Unfortunately, "religion" has not got a good name in popular thinking. Many feel there is far too much evidence that it tends to bring out the worst, rather than the best, in people, and causes so many to treat each other so badly.

A great deal of conflict in the world seems to have a religious basis – and while that is largely a matter of confrontation between people of different faiths (Christian, Muslim, Jewish, etc.), it does spill over also into people of different brands of Christianity – Northern Ireland being a most intractable example of that. The news media, when they deal with religious issues, tend to publicise conflicts between Christians, at local as well as national or international level. The public are conditioned to hearing about church affairs only when there are unsavoury things to report. No wonder religion then becomes a turn-off.

There is also a rather bemused attitude towards the authority that some religions seem to claim over the lives of their adherents. That just doesn't seem to fit in with the liberal attitudes of modern society towards people's private lives. Have churches and their leaders any legitimate authority to make pronouncements about sexual matters, contraception, homosexuality, or social issues like divorce and remarriage, and the rights of women, that are stricter than the laws of the land? Many Christians would say that a "Christian lobby" has considerable potential in bringing to the notice of elected leaders in parliament and local authorities principles that are very important for a caring society, and one in which all have freedom to pursue their own religion.

The character of Sunday has changed enormously during my lifetime in England. Many former restrictions on trading, sport and entertainment were based on an understanding that this is a Christian country, in which Sunday is a day of quiet, of prayer, of rest from secular work. Large numbers of citizens who were not regular churchgoers felt a certain sense of responsibility to uphold the traditional character of Sunday, and would not, for instance, disturb their neighbours by mowing their lawn on a Sunday, or having a bonfire, and certainly not by having a noisy party. Many respected the fact that the sight of washing hanging out on a Sunday was not liked by some who lived around them. Gradually Sunday has become more like other days. Some Christians fought against the Sunday opening of cinemas; more recently some fought very hard to "Keep Sunday Special", and tried to stop the deregulation of shopping hours.

However, a visit to any shopping centre on a Sunday shows that a clear case can be made out for shops being open at times when most people are not at work. I have strong reservations about the churches trying to resist public demand which makes sense. Of course it means that some people, working on Sunday to serve the public, cannot get to church services at the times when they usually are held – but that puts the ball in the church's court, to discern what provision for public worship is most appropriate, with regard both to the form it takes, and the day and time when it is offered. Actually, from the point of view of customers of shops, restaurants, etc. that are open on Sundays, and of people who attend or take part in sporting events, it should still often be possible to attend a church service as well. I don't think evangelism is helped by trying to restrict other things that are on offer on Sundays besides corporate Christian worship.

The churches shouldn't need "protectionism". Sunday Schools have certainly suffered from so many other activities being now available to children on Sundays. Christian parents have often had agonising decisions to make, when their children have wanted to join sports teams, etc. which would prevent them from joining in the provision made by their church for families with children. I note that churches now seem to refrain completely from complaining to the organisers of sports, car boot sales, dancing classes, and other things that "compete" with them on Sunday mornings – the battle, if there ever should have been one, is lost – we have to come to terms with society as it now is.

That should make churches extremely careful to ensure that what they offer to children is of a high enough standard. If ever youngsters came to church or Sunday School because there was nothing else to do, that was never a very strong or sound basis for building up a "junior church" that would lead on to enthusiasm to go further with Jesus in years to come.

While the drop in church attendance over the last few decades is naturally a cause for much regret among Christians, yet great encouragement can be found in the fact that in this day and age there are as many people as there are who are willing to go against the grain of society's attitudes, and bear witness to their Christian faith as practising members of the churches of Britain. God can use the few for the forwarding of his purposes, as the Bible and Christian history testify over and over again. If the few get even fewer, there can still be hope.

Transport and religion may seem rather strange things to put together in my memoirs as having been so prominent in my life and interests. One word that links them together in relation to modern developments is "Privatisation". Most travel in Britain is now by private car – and so people don't meet others in the course of their journeys in the way that public transport makes possible. All the cars rushing along the motorway come from different places and have different destinations; but for the "trunk" part of their journey they are closed boxes in very close proximity to other closed boxes, signalling to each other by means of indicator lights primarily, and just occasional hoots of the horn, or even worse "road-rage", if one driver thinks another is acting dangerously or selfishly.

Many would say that religion too is largely privatised now. For those whose Sunday worship amounts only to watching "Songs of Praise", there we have a "privatised" church. How nice not to have a collection bag, or the Vicar's notices about forthcoming jumble sales, with subtle pressure on people to do something more for the church than just to occupy a pew; how nice it can be too to "worship" in the comfort one's armchair in a cosy room, without having to wrap up for that chilly and draughty church.

And how nice not to have to expect to meet other worshippers and be polite to them even if one doesn't care for them much. "You can be a perfectly good Christian without going to Church" is a refrain that is so comforting to use, trying to evade all the challenges of serious Christian discipleship. If I had a pound for every time that, or a similar, remark has been made to me, I would be a good deal wealthier than I am. However, we must be glad that we live in a free country, and we must respect other people's freedom as we hope they will respect ours.

Transport and religion seem to be brought together in Sydney Carter's hymn from which the title of this book is taken; and I think we must read its words in whatever ways we feel we can best identify ourselves with them. I find that when I say them as a prayer, the "you" who recurs being an address to the God in whom I believe and trust, they express very well the philosophy behind the way I try to face life:

> One more step along the world I go,
> One more step along the world I go.
> From the old things to the new,
> Keep me travelling along with you.
> *And it's from the old I travel to the new;*
> *Keep me travelling along with you.*
>
> Round the corners of the world I turn;
> More and more about the world I learn.

All the new things that I see,
You'll be looking at along with me.
> *And it's from the old I travel to the new;*
> *Keep me travelling along with you.*

As I travel through the bad and good,
Keep me travelling the way I should.
Where I see no way to go,
You'll be telling me the way, I know.
> *And it's from the old I travel to the new;*
> *Keep me travelling along with you.*

Give me courage when the world is rough;
Keep me loving though the world is tough,
Leap and sing on all I do.
Keep me travelling along with you.
> *And it's from the old I travel to the new;*
> *Keep me travelling along with you.*

You are older than the world can be,
You are younger than the life in me.
Ever old and ever new,
Keep me travelling along with you.
> *And it's from the old I travel to the new;*
> *Keep me travelling along with you.*

Sydney Carter

(Reproduced by permission of Stainer & Bell Ltd.)